A Brief Guide to Florida's Monuments and Memorials

UNIVERSITY PRESS OF FLORIDA

Florida A&M University, Tallahassee
Florida Atlantic University, Boca Raton
Florida Gulf Coast University, Ft. Myers
Florida International University, Miami
Florida State University, Tallahassee
New College of Florida, Sarasota
University of Central Florida, Orlando
University of Florida, Gainesville
University of North Florida, Jacksonville
University of South Florida, Tampa
University of West Florida, Pensacola

A Brief Guide
to Florida's Monuments
and Memorials

Roberta Sandler

University Press of Florida

Gainesville · Tallahassee · Tampa · Boca Raton

Pensacola · Orlando · Miami · Jacksonville · Ft. Myers · Sarasota

12   11   10   09   08   6   5   4   3   2   1

LIBRARY OF CONGRESS CATALOGING-IN-PUBLICATION DATA
Sandler, Roberta, 1943–
A brief guide to Florida's monuments and memorials/Roberta Sandler.
p. cm.
Includes bibliographical references and index.
ISBN 978-0-8130-3258-0 (alk. paper)
1. Monuments—Florida—Guidebooks. 2. Memorials—Florida—Guidebooks.
3. Historic sites—Florida—Guidebooks. 4. Florida—History. I. Title.
F312.S36 2008
975.9—dc22   2008011013

All photographs are by Martin Sandler unless credited otherwise.

The University Press of Florida is the scholarly publishing agency for the State
University System of Florida, comprising Florida A&M University, Florida Atlantic
University, Florida Gulf Coast University, Florida International University, Florida
State University, New College of Florida, University of Central Florida, University
of Florida, University of North Florida, University of South Florida, and University
of West Florida.

University Press of Florida
15 Northwest 15th Street
Gainesville, FL 32611–2079
http://www.upf.com

In loving memory of my father, Leonard P. Haimes,
and my aunt, Ruth "Cookie" Halpert

Contents

1. Northwest Florida

2. Northeast Florida

3. Central East Florida

4. Southeast Florida

5. Southwest Florida

6. Central West Florida

7. Central Florida

Acknowledgments

I could not have written this book without the help of many people, but I wish to express my gratitude to several people in particular.

For guiding me around historic sites, I am indebted to the Zimmerman Agency in Tallahassee and especially to Beth LaCivita of Historic Florida Consulting.

A note of thanks to Georgia Turner of Georgia Turner Group for guiding me through sites in Daytona Beach and Polk County. Thanks to Stuart Newman and Associates for enabling me to visit Fort Jefferson.

I am grateful to Beth Davis for enlightening me about the fishing industry in Cedar Key. Thanks also to Lynne Robertson, chief curator of West Florida Historic Preservation, Inc.

Several historical societies were of help to me, including those in Fernandina Beach, Bartow and Dunedin.

Many convention and visitors bureaus generously led me to historic sites or provided valuable information. I especially wish to thank those in St. Augustine, Sarasota, Jacksonville, Bradenton, Fort Myers, Kissimmee, Orlando, Gainesville, Daytona Beach and those along Florida's freshwater frontier.

I must also thank Michelle Ferguson-Cohen, a descendant of Mariana Bonifay, for providing a copy of Bonifay's will. I am grateful to Sallie Worley, Tim Tetzlaff, James Durante, Ruth Pompey, Amber Costa, Al Hendry III, Harold Hayden Lundy and others for sharing their family histories.

Thanks to Virginia Snyder, Joan Matey, Charles Steadham and Bill Dreggors for giving me insight into the lives of George Morikami, Richard Ervin, Gamble Rogers and Lue Gim Gong, respectively.

I deeply appreciate the generous assistance of Tana Porter, research librarian at Orange County Regional History Center, and Frank Towers at Camp Blanding.

A special thanks to my sister-in-law Sandra Birnberg and my friends Emily Rosen, Judy Beatty and Troy Corley for understanding this project's enormity and for giving me needed encouragement.

Without the love and support of my husband, Marty, this project could never have been completed.

Finally, my thanks to the University Press of Florida for recognizing the great importance of Florida's monuments and memorials and for publishing this book.

Introduction

There are monuments and memorials throughout Florida.

They vary from obelisks and columns to stone boulders, murals, parks, churches and statues.

For the most part, they pay tribute to a significant event or to pioneers and relative newcomers from all backgrounds. They are reminders of people, places and moments that should never be forgotten.

The common denominator among these monuments and memorials is that they represent and honor people and events that had an impact on Florida's—and in some cases, the nation's—history.

For example, the monuments at Camp Blanding in Clay County memorialize World War II heroes who were camp trainees, many of whom parachuted into Normandy on D-Day in 1944.

A statue in Volusia County is dedicated to baseball legend Jackie Robinson, who played in the first racially integrated baseball game—and it took place here in Florida in 1946.

In St. Lucie County, a statue of CeeCee Ross Lyles honors the memory of a flight attendant and the passengers who were killed aboard United Flight 93 on September 11, 2001.

Florida's monuments and memorials were erected in memory of ordinary and extraordinary people: developers, conquistadors, astronauts, soldiers, farmers, fishermen, statesmen, teachers, inventors and others.

Florida also is home to several national monuments and memorials. These include the hideaway of a Confederate cabinet member; the site of the first French settlement in the New World; and the fort where Dr. Samuel Mudd was imprisoned for setting the broken leg of President Lincoln's assassin.

The purpose of this book is to encourage you to see Florida's monuments and memorials as more than stone boulders, bronze sculptures and granite slabs.

Who were these people immortalized in bronze? Where did they come from and why? What were their contributions? Why did they have a profound effect on others?

Why were certain events so momentous that they had to be inscribed in stone and bronze? How did these events change lives and put an indelible stamp on Florida's history?

As you will see, what makes these monuments and memorials intriguing and important are the stories behind them, stories of heroism, dedication, patriotism, daring, perseverance, love and tolerance.

Perhaps because they are small and rural, some Florida counties seem to have no monuments and memorials. Other counties, large and well populated, have many. The monuments included in this book are either unique or unusual. They are a sampling and do not comprise all of Florida's memorial sites.

I hope the monuments and memorials I have spotlighted will encourage you to explore and discover more of them and to learn their stories. They are windows into Florida's diverse and fascinating past.

Northwest Florida

Mariana Pingrow Bonifay Monument

Address: In the center of Garden Street, about one block west of St. Michael's Cemetery, Pensacola. Escambia County.

Mariana Bonifay lived by her own sense of independence. She left an indelible fingerprint on Pensacola history through her accomplishments and in a legacy of descendants who still live in Florida.

Mariana Pingrow Bonifay was born in 1760 in Nantes, France, an industrial and seaport city in the western Loire Valley. She sailed to Santo Domingo and married plantation owner Joseph Bonifay, with whom she had several children.

Mariana Bonifay may have fled from Santo Domingo to New Orleans after being warned by her maid that the plantation slaves were planning an uprising.

It is unclear whether Joseph Bonifay stayed behind in Santo Domingo or went with his wife to New Orleans; however, when she moved to Pensacola, she apparently did so without him. By 1784, she owned a house in Pensacola, according to West Florida Historic Preservation, Inc., a nonprofit organization of the University of West Florida. In 1801, Mariana received notice that Joseph had died the previous year.

The news may not have sent tears spilling down Mariana Bonifay's cheeks. At the time, she was involved in a relationship with Carlos (Charles) Lavalle, a Mobile, Alabama-born carpenter about twelve years her junior. She and Lavalle had several children together.

Mariana Pingrow Bonifay Monument. Photo courtesy of Lynne Robertson, chief curator, West Florida Historic Preservation, Inc.

In 1790, Bonifay and Lavalle started a real-estate business together in which they bought land, built houses on it, then rented or sold the properties. It was a lucrative venture. Today one of the houses, the 1805 Lavalle House, is open to the public and is part of Historic Pensacola Village, a collection of twenty properties in the Pensacola National Register Historic District.

In 1807, Bonifay and Lavalle bought a brickyard. Streets needed paving, and the couple turned the brickyard into another successful enterprise.

Bonifay and Lavalle ended their relationship by mutual consent around the year 1822. When Bonifay died, she was about sixty-nine years old. Lavalle lived for another twenty-five years. He died at the age of eighty-two.

Mariana Bonifay's will, dated September 16, 1825, lists her assets at the time of death, including real-estate properties, cattle, three male slaves and two female slaves. She placed a value of one hundred fifty dollars on her slave Pedro. To her daughter Josefa Candelaria, Mariana bequeathed the child of Sophia, one of Mariana's slaves.

Mariana also bequeathed one thousand dollars to her son Manuel for the lifetime care of his brother, Andres Antonio, who was deaf and dumb.

In 1967, Mariana Bonifay's descendants erected a monument to her. The granite monument is inscribed with a cross below which these words appear:

Mariana Pingrow Bonifay 1760–1829.
    Early Pensacola Pioneer.
    Born, Nantes, France. Married to Joseph Bonifay in Santo Domingo. Moved to Pensacola 1781, when its population was 250. Purchased first home on West Intendencia Street 1784. Left a widow by the death of her husband, she encountered many hardships. Her descendants were a third of Pensacola's population during the Civil War period.
    She was engaged in real estate and building, 1790–1807. In 1807, she received from Spain a land grand at Bohemia (Scenic Highway) and purchased the Bohemia Brickyard.
    Her son, Manuel, was associated with her until her death. . . . Another son, Joseph, helped her in a cattle and farming enterprise. The City of Bonifay, Florida, was named for her great-grandson, Judge Frank B. Bonifay.
    The history of Pensacola bears the impression of her wise, ambitious and tireless efforts in private and public life. She is best remembered as a loving mother of ten children who largely endowed Pensacola with its Spanish-French traditions.

T. T. Wentworth, Jr., Monument

Address: 103 S. Jefferson Street, Pensacola. (850) 595–5990. Escambia County.

In 1906, a young boy named Theodore Thomas Wentworth, Jr., was walking on a Pensacola beach when he spotted something shiny in the sand.

The curious eight-year-old picked up the object, brushed the sand from it and saw that it was an old one-dollar gold coin. That discovery marked the beginning of his lifelong penchant for collecting and his love of history.

There are collectors and then there are pack rats. In the kindest sense of the word, "pack rat" is an apt description of T. T. Wentworth, Jr. (1898–1989), an amiable man who spent his entire life searching for, and finding, collectible artifacts and items from West Florida.

A stone monument in front of the T. T. Wentworth, Jr., Florida State Museum pays tribute to him.

It states:

> T. T. Wentworth, Jr., for his efforts in preserving the historical treasures of the city of Pensacola. By Resolution of the City Council February 8, 1962.

Inside the museum, visitors come face to face with Wentworth's passion for finding, collecting and exhibiting things. The museum also gives insight into Wentworth's life and his accomplishments.

Theodore Thomas Wentworth, Jr., was born in Mobile, Alabama, in 1898 and moved with his family to Pensacola when he was a child. His industriousness began at age eight when he sold newspapers on the city's streets. As a young man, he found employment as an office boy, a telegraph messenger and as proprietor of a bicycle shop.

At age twenty-one, Wentworth became the youngest county commissioner in Florida. In 1928, he became Escambia County's tax collector.

Part of his duties as tax collector was selling license tags, of which there sometimes were leftovers. Wentworth added them to his private collection of items he had found and kept through the years.

T. T. Wentworth, Jr., Florida State Museum and Monument.

Wentworth enjoyed his greatest financial success as a real estate agent. Civic-minded, he pushed for the city to build roads and to advertise Pensacola as a tourist destination. He also was among the founders of the Pensacola Historical Society.

His greatest pleasure, however, may have come from amassing and displaying his personal collection, an eclectic assortment that wasn't necessarily valuable, but which he found intriguing.

Margaret Reining, a longtime volunteer at the T. T. Wentworth, Jr., Florida State Museum, recalls conversing with a visitor who said he knew Wentworth.

The visitor told Reining that whenever Wentworth found something of interest, he would peddle over to a building where he housed his collection. He used the building, a roadside museum in Ensley, Florida, to educate the public about Florida history.

Wentworth would sit down at his manual typewriter, type a description of the object he had found and put the treasure into a display case along with the accompanying description. He was reportedly offered one million dollars for the collection but turned down the offer.

Wentworth's collection eventually outgrew his building, so in 1983 he donated everything to the State of Florida. Officials were faced with a dilemma: Where would the state keep more than one hundred thousand items?

A solution presented itself when the city of Pensacola donated its historic city hall as a permanent museum site. Built circa 1907 in Renaissance Revival style, the three-story, sand-colored building on Jefferson Street bears a crest on top with the city's seal and the words "Pensacola, Florida." Today this elegant building welcomes thousands of visitors a year to view the rotating collections of the T. T. Wentworth, Jr., Florida State Museum.

Additional items from the Wentworth Collection are on exhibit in Historic Pensacola Village, a complex of historic buildings that includes five houses furnished from various time periods, from 1800 through the 1920s, as well as the Old Christ Church, the Museum of Industry and the Museum of Commerce. The outfitting of all these buildings would not have been possible without the T. T. Wentworth, Jr., Collection.

In a sense, says Margaret Reining, the T. T. Wentworth, Jr., Florida State Museum is Pensacola's attic, filled with Wentworth's sometimes-odd treasures. His collection includes a petrified cat, a giant shoe, an old telephone switchboard, antique telephones and clocks, old medicine bottles and thousands more items. In addition, the museum features a discovery gallery for children, changing exhibits and a permanent exhibit about the history of Florida.

T. T. Wentworth, Jr., died in 1989 at age ninety. He was a man who found value and enjoyment in preserving ordinary, and sometimes extraordinary, things.

William Allen "Uncle Bill" Lundy Monument

Address: Corner of Highway 85 and First Avenue (across from the Kentucky Fried Chicken), Crestview. Okaloosa County.

September 1, 1957, marked the demise of a man considered to be Florida's last surviving Confederate veteran. "Uncle Bill" Lundy was 109 years old.

Lundy's real name was William Allen Lundy, but "he probably got the nickname 'Uncle Bill' because he was kin to so many people," says his grandson Harold Hayden Lundy, who lives in Crestview and shares fond memories and family stories about "Uncle Bill."

Uncle Bill was born in Alabama in September 1848. By 1864, the Civil War was in its fourth year, and Uncle Bill, then sixteen years old, enlisted in the Fourth Alabama Cavalry in a unit called Brown's Home Guards, but he never fired a shot. A year later, the war ended.

William Allen "Uncle Bill" Lundy Monument with flagpole.

While Lundy's wartime service was brief, his duties put him in the path of potentially dangerous conflict. It was not something he dwelled on in his later years. "My grandpa didn't talk much about the Civil War," says Harold Hayden Lundy, "but on one occasion, we were driving from Florida into Alabama, and Grandpa pointed to a spot where there once was a wooden bridge that connected the two states.

"'I spent a lot of nights guarding that bridge,' Grandpa told me. He said, 'I was told not to shoot any Yankees unless they tried to burn the bridge.'" Evidently, Union soldiers did not brandish any lit matches on Uncle Bill's watch.

Years after the Civil War, toward the close of 1890, Uncle Bill moved to Okaloosa County. At the time, it was part of Walton County.

Harold Hayden says his grandmother, the former Mary Jane Lassiter, could not read, but she was a good home-maker who took care of four daughters and six sons while Uncle Bill farmed his land.

Uncle Bill grew blueberries on about twenty acres of Clear Springs land. Harold Hayden Lundy remembers that his grandpa also raised bees to sell honey and that Uncle Bill and one of his sons, Joseph "Joe" Jefferson Lundy (Harold Hayden's father), operated a gristmill. They ground corn for people who lived in the area.

Many stories about Uncle Bill were passed down in the Lundy family, including one of how his son Joe tried to teach the older Lundy how to drive a Model T Ford.

Seated behind the steering wheel with the motor running, Uncle Bill blew the car horn to let Grandma Lundy know she should open the farm gate; however, unable to stop the car, he plowed into the gate. This experience immediately convinced Uncle Bill that his horse and buggy were a more reliable means of transportation than was the newfangled automobile.

In addition to the occasional runaway Model T, there were plenty of chickens running around the Lundy farm. The chickens came in handy around dinnertime and per-haps were a secret to his longevity. "He didn't go to doctors," says his grandson. "If he was sick, he could make his own chicken soup."

Uncle Bill liked to hunt for deer and turkey and although he used a walking stick when he was old and white haired, he shot a deer in 1954. At the time, he was 106 years old.

Harold Hayden Lundy remembers his grandfather as a jolly, happy-go-lucky man who did not get angry. He retained his sense of humor up until the very end of his life. It is said that Uncle Bill was flirting with the nurses when he was hospitalized at age 109.

Harold Hayden Lundy chuckles: "Grandpa was friendly and he joked around. When I was a little boy, he'd put me in his lap and give me a big old hug and call me 'Little Billy,' even though he knew it wasn't my name."

Beneath a Confederate flag, a memorial stone stands in Confederate Park, a tiny patch of city land located in a traffic median in Crestview. The memorial, dedicated by the Crestview Lions Club in 1958, bears this inscription:

> Dedicated to "Uncle Bill" Lundy, Florida's last Confederate veteran, 1848–1957, and all Confederate soldiers of Florida.

Florida's First Confederate Monument

Address: In front of Walton County Courthouse, 571 Highway 90 East, DeFuniak Springs. (850) 892–8115. Walton County.

Confederate monuments and Confederate statues exist all around Florida, especially in courthouse squares, but what sets DeFuniak Springs' Confederate monument apart is that it was the first one erected in Florida.

Located next to a flagpole flying the Confederate flag, the marble obelisk-style monument is about five feet tall and is set on a three-tier base of about the same height.

The monument says,

> To the memory of the Confederate dead of Walton County, Florida. Erected by the Ladies of the Walton County Female Memorial Association. 1871.

Beneath the inscription there is a carving of two flag-draped cannons with cannon balls piled between them.

The monument lists the soldiers from Walton County who died during the Civil War. The list includes at least one father and son, eight members of the Gillis family, five members of the McLean family and several officers of the Sixth Florida Volunteers.

The monument originally was capped with a finger pointing to the sky to symbolize the slain soldiers' ascension into heaven. The finger is now missing.

A sign erected near the monument in 1967 by the Florida Board of Parks and Historic Memorials identifies the monument as "Florida's First Memorial Monument."

The Walton County Female Memorial Association paid $250 to commission the monument, which was placed at Valley Church in 1871. It was later moved to Eucheeanna, which was then the seat of Walton County. Subsequently, the monument was moved yet again, sparking a major controversy. Local historian William Steadley-Campbell, whose family has lived in the area since the early 1800s, recounts the events:

"When DeFuniak Springs replaced Eucheeanna as the county seat, an unknown person or persons stole the

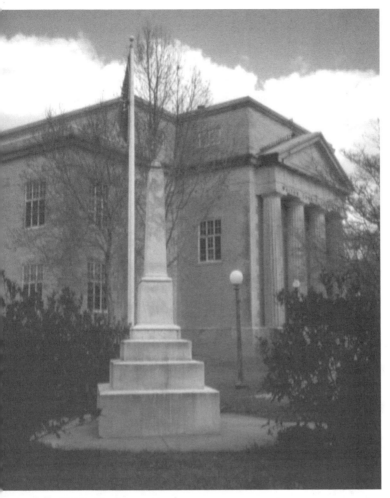

Florida's First Confederate Monument.

monument on a moonless night and brought it to DeFuniak Springs," says Steadley-Campbell. "There was almost
a shooting war over this act because both Eucheeanna
and DeFuniak Springs fought over who should keep the
monument."

The two towns settled their differences and agreed that
the monument should remain in DeFuniak Springs.

William "W. D." Chipley Monument

Address: 685 Seventh Street, Chipley. (850) 638–4157. Washington County.

Ask Floridians to name a Florida railroad pioneer. If they live in southwest Florida, they will probably reply, "Henry Plant." If they live in southeast Florida, they will probably reply, "Henry Flagler." If they live in northwest Florida, they will probably say, "W. D. Chipley."

William Dudley Chipley was born in Georgia in 1840 and grew up in Kentucky. During the Civil War, he fought for the Confederacy at Shiloh and Chickamauga, sustaining wounds during both battles, but after convalescing, he resumed his duties.

By the time W. D. Chipley was captured near Atlanta by Union forces and imprisoned, he had reached the rank of lieutenant colonel. After the war, he married Ann Elizabeth Billups, and they settled in Columbus, Georgia, before moving to Pensacola in 1876.

William "W. D." Chipley Monument.

After engaging in some unsuccessful businesses, W. D. Chipley became interested in railroads. He obtained a charter to build the Pensacola and Atlantic Railroad, and by 1883, it was chugging from Pensacola to Crestview, Marianna, Carrabelle and Tallahassee, as described by Florida historian M. C. Bob Leonard in "Florida of the Railroad Barons."

In 1885, the Pensacola and Atlantic Railroad became part of the Louisville and Nashville (L&N) Railroad, which merged with several railroads in 1982 to become Seaboard System Railroad, later the CSXT rail system.

Prior to the arrival of W. D. Chipley's railroad, Panhandle towns depended on riverboats to transport goods. With his train service hurdling rivers and connecting with trains on Florida's east coast, the sparsely settled landscape thickened. Rural Panhandle towns matured into busy lumber and farming communities.

The town of Orange, founded in 1882 in what is now Washington County, was renamed Chipley in his honor.

The Pensacola and Atlantic Railroad was a lifeline and an economic boon for area farmers. During pear season in 1893, Shear & Wolf, a pear-packing house in the city of Chipley, filled seven railway cars with 500 boxes of pears each.

That same year, local watermelon farmers filled railroad cars with their produce and sent them to market. In 1897, cotton producers in Chipley shipped nearly 1,500 bales of cotton by railroad. Local tobacco and sweet-potato farmers also relied on the railroad (Leonard, "William D. Chipley").

In addition to spurring west Florida's agricultural development by providing rail service, W. D. Chipley served as mayor of Pensacola and as state senator from 1895 to 1897. He also sat on the board of trustees of Stetson University and was a director of the Florida Chautauqua. He died in 1897 and was buried in Columbus, Georgia.

The citizens of Chipley erected a monument to W. D. Chipley. It is located, appropriately, by the town's railroad station. The monument is, in effect, a stone biography.

These words appear on the front:

William Dudley Chipley, 1840 to 1897. Builder of the Pensacola and Atlantic Railroad, beside which citizens of an infant city named Chipley in his honor.

These words appear on the sides:

Statesman: Florida. Democratic Chairman, State Senator, Mayor of Pensacola.

His influence was felt for years in Florida and sometimes national affairs. He came within one legislative vote of being elected to the U.S. Senate in 1897.

Public benefactor. Gave of his time, talent, and financial resources to numerous civic, religious, charitable and educational institutions, many of which he served as a trustee or other officer.

There is a taller, more elaborate monument to W. D. Chipley in Plaza Ferdinand in Pensacola.

Union Soldier Monument

Address: Corner of Eighth Street and Georgia Avenue, Lynn Haven. Bay County.

It is estimated that during the American Civil War, more than six hundred thousand Union and Confederate soldiers lost their lives. Of the approximately 2.5 million men enrolled in the Union army, about three hundred sixty thousand were killed in action or died during imprisonment or from other causes, notes Dick Weeks in "The Price in Blood! Casualties in the Civil War."

Sometimes Union forces were obliterated in the blink of an eye. In an 1864 battle, for example, the First Maine Heavy Artillery lost more than two-thirds of its men in seven minutes. More commonly, losses were cumulative, such as those

Union Soldier Monument.

suffered by the Union's Irish Brigade, whose soldiers hailed from Massachusetts, Pennsylvania, and New York. By the war's end, the Irish Brigade had lost about 85 percent of its men. Either way, the death toll was staggering.

When the war ended in 1865, surviving Union soldiers wearily returned to their homes up North. However, due to emergence of an organization that offered support to former Union soldiers, many of these veterans would eventually pick up roots and move to Florida.

Headquartered in Illinois, this organization was the Grand Army of the Republic (GAR) and it was open only to honorably discharged Union veterans.

In the first decade of the 1900s, Union veterans, enticed by advertisements in the GAR's *National Tribune*, bought lots in St. Cloud in Osceola County, Florida, and built modest retirement homes there.

Union army veteran W. H. Lynn, publisher of the *National Tribune*, also promoted a little community in Bay County in Florida's Panhandle, where veterans could buy 50' × 50' lots for $150. That community was Lynn Haven.

It would be nearly ninety years before the film *Field of Dreams* popularized the phrase, "If you build it, they will come," but Lynn Haven must have been W. H. Lynn's field of retirement dreams because he helped build it, and the veterans came.

The veterans erected a GAR hall and each month they set aside money from their pension checks to pay for the construction of a town monument dedicated to all Union veterans.

It took several years before they had amassed enough money, but finally, in 1920, Lynn Haven's residents commissioned a company in Salem, Ohio, to create the monument.

That same year, as proud onlookers gathered in a Lynn Haven park, W. W. Krape, serving his last year as mayor of Lynn Haven, dedicated the completed monument to all Union soldiers, living or deceased.

The city of Lynn Haven claims that this is the only such monument south of the Mason-Dixon line to pay tribute to Union soldiers.

The statue features a Union soldier facing north and holding a musket. He stands on a three-tier, forty-foot-high pedestal engraved "1920. GAR."

Above this information, an inscription states:

Monument in memory of the Union soldiers of the Civil War—1861–1865.

The monument was later rededicated to the memory of all American veterans killed in battle.

1838 Constitution Convention State Memorial and Museum

Address: 200 Allen Memorial Way (off U.S. 98), Port St. Joe. (850) 222–8029. Gulf County.

The 1838 Constitution Convention State Memorial is surely one of Florida's most beautiful monuments. Made of marble and supported by two marble columns, the memorial bears the banner words, "1838 Florida Constitution."

The memorial commemorates the birth of the state of Florida and honors the fifty-six territorial delegates who drafted Florida's first constitution. It is inscribed:

> The Assembly of the First Constitutional Convention of this state convened in a building that was standing on this spot in 1838.

The memorial also bears these words:

> All men are equal before the law and have certain inalienable rights among which are those of enjoying and defending life and liberty, acquiring possessions and protecting property and pursuing happiness and obtaining safety.
>
> State Constitution Memorial Commission. Cary A. Hardee, Governor; H. Clay Crawford, Secretary of State; Rivers Buford, Attorney General. 1922.

Located near the memorial, the Constitution Convention State Museum recreates the historic convention hall and features audio-animated "delegates" who tell the story of the convention.

That story begins in 1838, when the delegates met in St. Joseph for their convention. The town was a bustling seaport. Today, it no longer exists. (Apalachicola's increasing desirability as a trading port and the yellow-fever epidemic of 1841 caused St. Joseph's population to dwindle. A hurricane that hit St. Joseph in September 1844 was a death knell for the town.)

On December 3, 1838, the delegates began drafting a constitution in anticipation of the territory of Florida becoming a state. Leading the delegation as president was Robert Reid, a delegate from St. Johns.

Other delegates included Samuel Parkhill, Thomas M. Blount, James D. Westcott, George E. McClellan, William P. Duval (a future territorial governor of Florida), Thomas Baltzell and William Wyatt.

There are several interesting bits of trivia concerning the delegates. About six years prior to the convention, in 1832, Baltzell, an attorney, wounded Westcott in a duel in Alabama. Presumably, the wound was not life threatening because Westcott did not die until 1880, outliving Baltzell by fourteen years, according to Lawrence Kestenbaum's Political Graveyard history site.

Another notable delegate was Wyatt, of Leon County. His daughter Mary married William Whitaker, Sarasota's first permanent white settler. According to the Sarasota County Historical Resources department, the Whitakers' daughter Nancy was the first white child born in Sarasota.

The delegation drafted the constitution by splitting into eighteen committees, each familiar with a specific area of government and using other Southern states' constitutions as guidelines.

1838 Constitution Convention State Memorial.

Although the convention produced a complete draft only thirty-four days after it convened, it took almost seven years before the U.S. Congress passed an act that admitted Florida into the Union. On March 3, 1845, Florida became America's twenty-seventh state.

Congressional procedure at the time required that a Northern state be admitted simultaneously with a Southern state, so that year Iowa also entered the Union.

Among the seventeen articles the delegates drew up, Article XVI states that the General Assembly cannot pass laws that emancipate slaves, cannot prohibit immigrants to Florida from bringing their slaves with them and can pass laws preventing free blacks from immigrating to Florida.

Article XVI reflected the times. Fortunately, those times are gone.

Captain John Parkhill Monument

Address: In front of the old Capitol on 400 South Monroe Street, overlooking Apalachee Parkway, Tallahassee. Leon County.

Under the Indian Removal Act, which President Andrew Jackson signed into federal law in 1830, all Native American tribes east of the Mississippi had to relocate west of the river. Those tribes included Seminoles living in Florida.

The three Seminole Wars, fought in Florida between 1817 and 1858, never fully accomplished this goal.

In November 1857, during the Third Seminole War (1855–58), thirty-four-year-old captain John Parkhill, from Leon County, led a company of about 110 Florida Volunteers

Captain John Parkhill Monument.

on a mission to round up Florida's remaining Seminoles and Miccosukees. Seminole War historian Chris Kimball describes the campaign in detail in his article, "The Last Battle of the Third Seminole War."

Captain Parkhill and his men arrived at a cypress swamp in what is now Collier County, in southwest Florida, and trekked along a trail of recently abandoned Seminole villages.

Indeed, notes Kimball, the Seminoles always seemed to be one step ahead of the U.S. Army, and the Indians' familiarity with the territory's hiding places afforded them an advantage over their white pursuers. There were times when the Florida Volunteers' scout did not seem to know where he was.

During their search, Parkhill and his men came upon Royal Palm Hammock, an abandoned Indian village.

The Seminoles' staple crops of pumpkins, potatoes, corn and rice filled the village landscape, but the soldiers quickly razed these fields. If the Seminoles came back, they would find nothing to return to.

It was shortly after Thanksgiving Day that Parkhill and his men made camp in the area. Leaving his company to rest, Parkhill and about thirty men set off to search along some trails. On one trail, they discovered tracks.

Had Parkhill then gone back to camp to summon the rest of his command, he may have fared better. Instead, he and his men went forward a few more miles. They arrived at a stream amid a cypress swamp.

Suddenly, dozens of Seminole warriors ambushed the small band of soldiers. Parkhill fell at the first volley of shots and died within minutes. The Seminoles fled, and the soldiers, although most were wounded, managed to get back to camp with the lifeless body of their captain.

The soldiers buried Captain Parkhill by a lakeside. For the Florida Volunteers, who looked on their leader with great fondness and admiration, Parkhill's death was a severe blow. The army decided not to pursue the fleeing Seminoles.

For the Seminoles, the incident at Royal Palm Hammock was a victory, notes Kimball. Within months, the Third Seminole War ended, having failed its objective. The remaining Seminoles, who had defended their right to remain in the land they called home, were never captured or removed from Florida.

Nobody knows where the remains of Captain Parkhill are interred, and it would be a notable postscript to the history of the Seminole Wars if his burial spot could be found. Most likely, Kimball and other historians surmise, the grave is in Fakahatchee Strand Preserve State Park or in Collier-Seminole State Park.

Palm Hammock was the site of the final battle of the Seminole Wars. Every February, the Royal Palm Hammock skirmish is reenacted at Collier-Seminole State Park as part of the Native American and Pioneer Festival.

A monument in front of the old Capitol in Tallahassee pays homage to the fallen hero of Palm Hammock. The monument is inscribed:

> Captain John Parkhill of Leon Volunteers. This monument is erected by his fellow citizens of Leon County, Florida, as a testimonial of their high esteem for his character and public services.
>
> He was born July 10, 1823, and was killed at Palm Hammock in South Florida while leading his Company in a charge against the Seminole Indians, November 28, A.D. 1857.

Natural Bridge Monuments

Address: Natural Bridge Battlefield Historic State Park, off SR 363, 7502 Natural Bridge Road, near Woodville. (850) 922–6007. Leon County.

Tallahassee was the only Confederate capital east of the Mississippi to successfully resist capture by Union forces during the Civil War.

The city earned that distinction after a battle waged along a naturally formed bridge near Tallahassee on March 6, 1865. The battle pitted about one thousand Union soldiers against five hundred to seven hundred Confederates.

The Union forces were led by naval commander William Gibson, who led his flotilla into Apalachee Bay, on the Gulf Coast, in early March 1865. Although Commander Gibson's men captured a bridge near St. Marks Lighthouse on March 3, his gunboats ran aground the following day. For two days, they were stuck in the St. Marks River.

This delay gave the Confederates, under the command of General William Miller, time to prepare a strategy to defend the capital of Tallahassee.

Young cadets from West Florida Seminary and old men recovering from battle wounds voluntarily joined General Miller's troops and confronted the Union enemy along Natural Bridge, on the St. Marks River, early on the morning of March 6. The fighting lasted about ten hours.

The Second and Ninety-ninth U.S. Colored Infantry were among Union troops at the Battle of Natural Bridge. (A summary of Natural Bridge and other Civil War battles fought in Florida can be found on the State of Florida Web site, Florida in the Civil War.)

While three Confederate soldiers died in the battle and another twenty-two suffered injuries, the casualties were much greater for the Union's side: twenty-one killed, eighty-nine wounded and dozens captured. The estimated casualties on the Confederate side totaled about twenty-six, according to statistics provided by American Civil War.com.

General John Newton, the Union army commander, could not penetrate the Confederate defense. Unable to

Natural Bridge Monument.

cross the St. Marks River via Natural Bridge to march on Tallahassee, he ordered his men to retreat. Tallahassee remained in Confederate hands.

Several monuments at Natural Bridge Battlefield Historic State Park pay tribute to the battle. The most prominent is a tall, white granite monument that rises from a three-tier granite base. A granite flag is draped across the top.

Two phrases—"In loving memory" and "Defenders of Natural Bridge. Lest we forget"—are featured above and beneath a design of two crossed muskets.

Also carved into the monument are these words:

This monument erected . . . as a . . . tribute of the People of Florida to commemorate the victory of the Battle of Natural Bridge, March 6, 1865, and to keep in cherished memory those brave men and boys who, in the hour of sudden danger, rushed from home and field and from the West Florida Seminary and joining a few disciplined troops by their united valor and patriotism, saved their capital from their invaders.

Tallahassee, being the only capital of the South not captured by the enemy during the War between the States.

One side of the monument lists the commands taking part in the Battle of Natural Bridge including:

Gen. William Miller in command; Col. George W. Scott's Cavalry; Col. Samuel Love's Militia; Col. C. W. DuPont, the Gadsden Grays; . . . the West Florida Cadets, the baby corps young as the youngest who wore the gray . . .

Other forces involved in the battle included Confederate major general Sam Jones; Company A, Milton Light Artillery; Dunham's Battery; and Abell's Battery.

A monument was placed at the Natural Bridge site by the United Daughters of the Confederacy, "in grateful memory of Col. George W. Scott and his gallant men."

Another monument bearing the flags of the United States and the Confederate States of America was dedicated in 2000. It honors "the Confederate and Union soldiers who were killed in action or later died from their wounds" at the Battle of Natural Bridge.

A third monument declares: "This stone is presented by J. B. Fletcher and Comrades in memory of Col. J. J. Daniels' Regiment of 1st Florida Reserves, and Col. Geo. W. Scott 5th Fla. Battalion of Cavalry who was in this battle March 6, 1865. J. B. Fletcher."

On the weekend closest to March 6 every year, a reenactment of the Battle of Natural Bridge takes place at Natural Bridge Battlefield Historic State Park.

Ed Ball Monument

Address: Ed Ball Wakulla Springs Lodge and State Park, 550 Wakulla Park Drive, Wakulla Springs. (850) 561–7217. Wakulla County.

He was a big, scary alien. He was half reptile, half human. He was the title character from the 1954 cult classic, *Creature from the Black Lagoon.*

Scientists in the film discover the creature while exploring a legendary lagoon near the Amazon River; however, what audiences of the 1950s didn't know was that the fabled "Black Lagoon" they saw onscreen was really Wakulla Springs, Florida. Today the Florida Department of Environmental Protection describes Wakulla Springs as "a pre–Ice Age sinkhole connected to an underground cave, and one of the world's largest, deepest freshwater springs."

Prior to the making of *Creature from the Black Lagoon,* a series of famous films was shot at this same Florida location. As alligators lazed beneath him, Olympic swimmer Johnny Weissmuller swung from a palm tree while filming early "Tarzan" movies at Wakulla Springs. Just as they would in Eisenhower's day, audiences of the 1930s readily believed that they were seeing a jungle river.

What does all this film trivia have to do with a memorial to an influential figure in Florida business and politics? The answer is that Wakulla Springs Lodge is located in Wakulla Springs State Park, and behind the lodge, a stone monument bears these words:

> Edward Ball. 1888 to 1981. Industrialist, naturalist, conservationist who for 40 years preserved and maintained the amenities of Wakulla Springs in a natural state, thus establishing a heritage for the preservation of these resources and the continued enjoyment and pleasure of those who followed.
>
> Dedicated in memory of Edward Ball by the state of Florida Department of Natural Resources, Division of Recreation and Parks, May 1997.

Edward ("Ed") Ball was born in Northumberland County, Virginia in 1888. His father was a prominent attorney. His

Ed Ball Monument.

family lineage included George Washington's mother, Mary Ball Washington, according to historical records from the Robert E. Lee Memorial Association.

Ball was a developer and financier. In 1937, he built the Wakulla Springs Lodge on property that he had bought and developed in the Florida Panhandle. The property included the springs.

Ball had a close hand in the design and furnishing of the twenty-seven-room, two-story lodge, which combines a Spanish-Moorish style with Art Deco details. Wakulla Springs Lodge and State Park are on the National Register of Historic Places. The park is a National Natural Landmark.

Ball's business acumen made him a multimillionaire. He owned vast amounts of land, as well as many railroads and banks, and was a cofounder of the St. Joe Paper Company.

In 1921, Ball's sister Jessie became the third wife of Alfred I. du Pont, heir to a gunpowder fortune. When du Pont died in 1935, Ed Ball assumed management of du Pont's trusts and, by investing the trusts' income, he vastly increased their value, according to the Edward Ball Papers, a collection held at the University of Florida.

When Ball died in 1981, he was ninety-three years old. According to his obituary in the *New York Times* on July 1, 1981, he "oversaw growth of that [Alfred du Pont] estate from an estimated $30 million when Mr. du Pont died in 1935, into a holding of some $2 billion."

Ed Ball was a businessman and a conservationist, as well as a philanthropist. The obituary states that he willed most of his seventy-five-million-dollar estate to the care and treatment of crippled children in Florida.

John Gorrie Memorial and State Museum

Address: Sixth Street, one block off U.S. 319–98, Apalachicola. (850) 653–1209. Franklin County.

When the weather is hot and humid, we Americans turn on the air conditioners in our cars, homes and offices. For that convenience we can thank John Gorrie, "the Father of Air-Conditioning."

In the charming Gulf Coast fishing village of Apalachicola, three notable reminders pay tribute to John Gorrie's importance: his gravesite, a monument to him, and the John Gorrie State Museum. The museum divulges his life story.

Born in 1803, Gorrie was raised in South Carolina and attended medical school in Fairfield, New York. In 1833, the thirty-year-old doctor moved to the seaport of Apalachicola.

In 1838, Gorrie married Caroline Myrick Beman, a widow who owned a hotel in Apalachicola. Together, they had a son and a daughter.

In addition to practicing medicine, Gorrie was a vital member of the Apalachicola community. He served variously as postmaster, city treasurer, mayor, president of a local bank, partner in a local hotel, justice of the peace and as a founder of Trinity Episcopal Church.

Gorrie had an interest in tropical diseases but, like his contemporaries in the medical field, he was unsure how the diseases were transmitted. In 1841, the dreaded yellow fever came to the Gulf Coast. Gorrie noticed that yellow fever seemed prevalent during summertime. Perhaps the disease needed heat to proliferate. If so, might cooler temperatures have an opposite effect?

Gorrie theorized that if patients were kept in a cold room where heat and humidity could be lowered, the patients' fevers would go down. He conducted an experiment. He sealed the doors and windows in a room, then hung a bowl of ice from the ceiling.

He covered the bowl with a hood containing a vent pipe that went through the ceiling into the chimney. As the ice melted, the air coming through the vent pipe cooled the

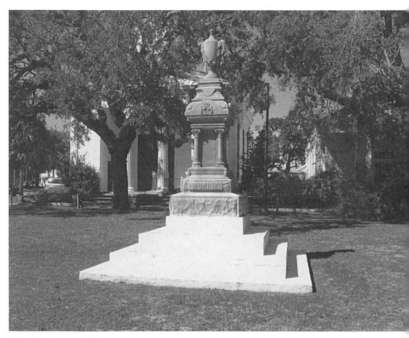

John Gorrie Memorial.

room. This was the method Gorrie used to bring down the fevers of his yellow-fever patients.

As writer George Chapel describes in his essay "Dr. John Gorrie: Refrigeration Pioneer," ice was available for sale in the Gulf Coast by the 1840s, albeit for a handsome price. Wealthy Floridians could order ice from suppliers in northern states, where it was cut from frozen lakes and preserved in underground icehouses, then wrapped in sawdust to keep it frozen during transport to Florida. Available at Gulf Coast docks in the blistering heat of summer, the precious northern ice found its way into cool drinks, ice-cream-making machines and into the rooms of Dr. Gorrie's patients.

In addition to using natural ice, Gorrie experimented in the hope of creating a machine that could make artificial ice. After toiling for years, he was able to build a rudimentary ice-making machine for which he obtained a U.S. patent around the year 1850; however, he had little success in finding financial backing.

Gorrie died in 1855, never knowing that his invention would be followed by more sophisticated refrigeration and air-conditioning machines that would change the world.

Today visitors to the John Gorrie Museum can view a replica of the ice machine that Gorrie built (the original model is on display at the Smithsonian Institute, in Washington, D.C.). His grave is across the street on a brick platform.

A monument to Gorrie stands on the grounds of Trinity Episcopal Church, on Sixth Street. The base of the monument says simply, "Gorrie."

The monument itself resembles an urn and bears the inscription:

This monument was erected by the Southern Ice Exchange in 1899.

Further, it is dedicated to a "pioneer who devoted his talents to the benefit of mankind."

The State of Florida honored John Gorrie by placing his statue in Statuary Hall at the U.S. Capitol.

Richard W. Ervin Monument

Address: Between Third and Fourth streets and NW Avenue A on U.S. 98, Carrabelle. Franklin County.

As described in documents in the Florida Supreme Court Library, it was not until 1949 that justices began wearing robes on the bench of Florida's Supreme Court. Previously, they had worn business suits. This sartorial switch was a notable one for chief justices of the time, including Justice Richard W. Ervin, whose sense of humor revealed itself when he commented on the black robe he was required to wear:

"It always seemed incongruous to me, a Florida Cracker born in Carrabelle, that I should be enrobed. I was awfully glad we weren't bewigged!" (More information about the

Richard W. Ervin Monument.

"Robe-Shy Judge" can be found online at flcourts.org, under the Florida Supreme Court Portrait Gallery.)

In 1975, the Florida Woodmen, a state chapter of an American fraternal organization, erected a monument in memory of Ervin that stands along U.S. 98 in Carrabelle. The inscription succinctly describes Ervin's concern for Florida's legal system and for his fellow man:

> Richard W. Ervin: Lawyer, jurist, fraternalist. Born in Carrabelle January 26, 1905. Destined to become one of Florida's most outstanding public servants, from legislative clerk in 1921 to Attorney General 1949–1964, to Supreme Court Justice 1964–1975, Chief Justice 1969–1970, National Director of Woodmen of the World, 1954–1975.
>
> Defender of the weak and helpless, advocate for education, knowledge and recognition of the rights of others.

Members of Woodmen of the World pledge themselves to projects that will benefit their fellow man. Richard Ervin marched to the beat of that pledge.

Ervin was born in Carrabelle and came from a family of lawyers and judges. He graduated from the University of Florida College of Law in 1928. Between 1929 and 1935, he practiced law in Pinellas, Lee and Putnam counties.

Then he turned his attention to political office. He served as attorney for the State Road Department (now Florida Department of Transportation) and as attorney for the Department of Public Safety.

In 1949, Ervin became attorney general of Florida, a position he held for the next fifteen years.

As attorney general, Ervin set his sights on eliminating Florida's organized bookmaking and illegal gambling activities; for this effort, the Junior Chamber of Commerce named him Florida's outstanding government official in 1950.

In 1959, Ervin became president of the National Association of Attorneys General, and five years later, Governor Farris Bryant appointed him to the Supreme Court of Florida.

Ervin became chief justice in 1969. During his years on

the bench, he wrote more than six hundred opinions, including two hundred dissents, notes the *Florida Bar News*.

Law clerk David Busch commented about Justice Ervin's dissents: " I began to appreciate . . . the special burden he carried by being someone out of step, many of us believe a step ahead of his peers." Busch's comments were included in an oral history program conducted on October 24, 1986 by the Florida Supreme Court Historical Society to honor Richard W. Ervin.

One of Ervin's dissents involved the 1972 law that restored the state's death penalty. Ervin opined that in certain cases, when sentencing judges decide who will get death, "we know intuitively who will [be sentenced]: the poor, the underprivileged, the public defender clients, the blacks and other minority people." He noted that "the affluent usually escape the death penalty."

With obvious admiration, David Busch observed this about Ervin:

> He kept his vocabulary as sharp as his pencil with daily working of crossword puzzles, and when it came time to give expression to majority opinion or his dissenting decision, his words appeared to flow effortlessly on the paper. (Florida Supreme Court Portrait Gallery)

After retiring from the court, Ervin continued to practice law. He died in 2004 at age ninety-nine.

Jefferson County High School (George Taylor) Monument

Address: 425 W. Washington Avenue (U.S. 90), Monticello. Jefferson County.

Among the most striking buildings in northwest Florida is the former Jefferson Academy, in Monticello. Built in the mid-1800s, the majestic Greek Revival–style building originally operated as a private school and became part of the county school system in 1889. It later became Monticello High School and then Jefferson County High School. The building is on the National Register of Historic Places. At present it is not in use due to structural weaknesses.

In the front of the high school, a stone monument reads:

> Jefferson County High School. Erected 1852. Charter granted in 1832 by Legislative Council. First brick school building constructed in state. Bricks made on George Taylor plantation. Building constructed . . . with slave labor. This memorial presented by senior class 1955.

George Taylor's plantation, a few miles west of Monticello on U.S. 90, still operates today as a working farm. His descendants grow soybeans and peanuts.

Among the descendents living in Monticello is Sallie Worley, Taylor's great-granddaughter and keeper of the Taylor family records. Those documents include receipts for the slaves whom George Taylor bought.

It is possible that the white-brick school building that has stood on U.S. 90 in Monticello for more than 150 years was built by some of the slaves listed on the receipts.

In addition to preserving rare documents, such as the slave receipts, Worley serves as her family's historian. Her summary of George Taylor's life is full of intriguing facts and amusing anecdotes.

George Washington Taylor was born in North Carolina in 1820 and died in Monticello in 1893. When he was a young boy, his parents decided to move to Florida, but his father died en route. The family pressed on and settled in Florida, where his widowed mother raised Taylor and his six brothers.

Jefferson County High School (George Taylor) Monument.

Although George Taylor was a cotton and corn farmer, he served at various times as sheriff of Jefferson County, tax collector and county commissioner. He was so liked and trusted that he was elected sheriff when he was only nineteen years old.

In 1843, Taylor married Susan Ellen West. After she died, he remarried, but he was widowed again. The first two marriages produced two surviving children.

Taylor had his Confederate uniform ready when the Civil War broke out in 1861 but he was persuaded, probably by his family, to remain at home to help his neighbors tend to their farms. He knew how difficult daily life would be for farm wives whose husbands were away at war.

In 1878, Taylor married his third wife, Sarah Johnson Raysor, who was twenty-three years his junior. She was the widow of Michael Raysor, a Confederate soldier killed during the war.

In 1881, Sarah gave birth to a daughter, Sarah Amanda, Sallie Worley's grandmother. George Taylor was sixty-one years old.

As a child, Sarah Amanda rode sidesaddle for three miles to get from the plantation to her school. After the Emancipation Proclamation, slavery was abolished at the plantation and hired farmhands continued to work Taylor's land. She once sucked poison from the wound of a black farmhand, thus saving his life. In gratitude, he gifted her with a live chicken every Christmas.

When George Taylor died, Sarah Amanda found herself in charge of running her father's plantation. She caused a touch of scandal in the family when she married DeWitt Kuder in 1910. He was from Toledo, Ohio, which meant that he was a Yankee!

Sarah Amanda had a gregarious personality, as family anecdotes reveal. One time, for example, a police officer pulled Sarah Amanda over for driving a mere three miles per hour. She explained that she had to drive slowly in order to stop and talk to everyone.

Sarah Amanda died in 1955. She left behind a historic working farm site and a legacy of treasured stories, which Sallie Worley delights in recounting.

These stories not only confirm the colorfulness of Sarah Amanda's personality, they also reflect a Florida of long ago, when a horse and buggy was the usual mode of transportation and plantations dotted the bucolic landscape.

Four Freedoms Monument

**Address: Four Freedoms Park, U.S. 90, opposite Madison
County Courthouse, Madison. Madison County.**

December 7, 1941. President Franklin Delano Roosevelt
called it "a day that will live in infamy."

Every American knows that the sudden attack on Pearl
Harbor, Hawaii, on December 7 by Japanese warplanes precipitated America's entry into World War II; however, here
is a question that few Americans can answer:

Who was the first American military hero killed in action
after December 7?

You'll find the answer at two sites in Madison, Florida:
Four Freedoms Park, where a monument is dedicated to
Captain Colin P. Kelly, Jr., and Oak Ridge Cemetery, where
Kelly is buried.

Colin P. Kelly, Jr., was born in Monticello, Florida, in 1915.
According to writer Jane Comer in "A Hero Remembered,"
Kelly graduated West Point in 1937 and was subsequently
assigned to Randolph Field in San Antonio.

On December 8, 1941, one day after Pearl Harbor was
attacked, Japanese aircraft bombed Clark Field near Manila,
in the Philippines. On December 10, Capt. Kelly, a pilot
with the Nineteenth Bombardier Group, was given orders to
attack Formosan airfields.

While piloting his B-17 toward Formosa, Kelly and his
crew flew over enemy ships, one of which appeared to be a
Japanese battleship.

As described by writer John Frisbee, Kelly requested
permission to drop his plane's three 600–pound bombs on
the enemy ships. After receiving two stand-by orders, Kelly
gave his bombardier the go-ahead. From more than twenty
thousand feet above the water, it appeared to the plane's
crew as though two of the bombs had struck the battleship.

Kelly steered his B-17 back toward Clark Field. En route,
enemy fighters suddenly appeared behind Kelly's B-17. One
of the fighters, a Mitsubishi A6M2 Zero, was piloted by
Saburo Sakai, a legendary fighter pilot of samurai ancestry
who laid claim to dozens of aerial victories. (In a strange

Four Freedoms Monument.

twist, Sakai, who survived the aerial battle, later lent his signature to a series of limited-edition lithographs of Kelly's famous aircraft, sold by the American art firm Air Art Northwest, whose Web site provides a detailed account of Kelly's heroic mission).

The Zeros fired on Kelly's B-17, killing one crewmember and wounding another. The B-17 caught on fire, and the flames quickly spread. Kelly may have sensed his impending doom but he remained at the controls. He ordered his copilot and crew to bail out immediately.

With difficulty, the crew parachuted from the enveloping flames just before the B-17 exploded in the skies. Kelly was still at the controls. The plane was only a few miles from Clark Field.

Of the surviving crewmembers, the copilot was badly burned, and the belly gunner was captured by the Japanese and spent more than three years as a POW. Kelly, a dark-haired, handsome twenty-six-year-old with a wife and a young son, had gone down with his plane.

At first, Kelly was credited with having sunk the battleship *Haruna*. Later, after the end of World War II, it was determined that he had actually attacked a light cruiser, the *Ashigara*.

Nevertheless, only three days after the attack on Pearl Harbor, Kelly became the first American hero of World War II. He was posthumously awarded the Distinguished Service Cross.

Nearly one year before the attack on Pearl Harbor, in his annual State of the Union address to Congress on January 6, 1941, President Roosevelt articulated the concept of the "Four Freedoms" that people everywhere should enjoy: Freedom of Speech, Freedom of Worship, Freedom from Want and Freedom from Fear. They represented America's ideals.

After Kelly's death, Roosevelt commissioned sculptor Walter Russell to sculpt a Four Freedoms Monument in memory of the young captain who had died protecting those freedoms.

Walter Russell's monument depicts four angels whose upraised wings represent those freedoms. The monument was dedicated to Captain Kelly in a ceremony at Madison Square Garden in New York City in 1943, before 60,000 people. It was re-dedicated in 1944 at a ceremony in Four Freedoms Park, in Madison, Florida.

Listening to their radios, people across the country were aural spectators at the dedication ceremony in which Florida governor Spessard Holland spoke. Kelly's mother voiced her thoughts that day: "Not only is the statue dedicated to my son, but to all those boys of the Allied nations who have given their lives" (Comer).

Not long after Kelly's Four Freedoms monument was installed in northern Florida, in 1945, citizens on the other side of the country, in Eugene, Oregon, were searching for a namesake for their new middle school. Learning of the young captain's heroism, they named the school Colin P. Kelly, Jr., Middle School.

Incidentally, the city of Madison, Florida, is the final resting place of another "first" war hero who, like Kelly, held the rank of captain. In 1861, Richard G. Bradford became the first Confederate officer from Florida to die in the Civil War.

Bradford perished while engaged in the Battle of Santa Rosa Island in an attempt to capture Fort Pickens from Union forces. Bradford County was named for him.

Stephen Foster Folk Culture Center State Park

Address: U.S. 41, White Springs. (386) 397–2733.
www.floridastateparks.org/stephenfoster. Hamilton County.

"Way Down Upon the Pedee River" didn't sound catchy enough to composer Stephen Foster.

That's when the Pennsylvania native turned to a north Florida river for inspiration and changed the lyrics of his tune "Old Folks at Home" to "Way Down Upon the Swannee River." Foster removed the *u* from Suwannee, notes the online guide to the Florida state park named in his honor.

The story of how a song about a meandering Southern river became an All-American classic begins, fittingly enough, on July 4. On that day in 1826 the nation mourned the deaths of John Adams and Thomas Jefferson, who died within hours of each other.

That same day, in Lawrenceville, Pennsylvania, William and Eliza Foster celebrated the birth of their ninth child, Stephen Collins Foster.

As a youth, Stephen Foster enjoyed singing and composing. He sold his first song when he was eighteen. In 1848, while working as a bookkeeper in Cincinnati, he had his first hit with "Oh! Susanna," sung by the Christy Minstrels, who were blackface entertainers. He was twenty-two.

The songwriter enjoyed a string of successes between 1850 and 1860, including "Camptown Races," "My Old Kentucky Home," "Jeanie with the Light Brown Hair," "Old Black Joe" and "Beautiful Dreamer."

He is best remembered for composing "Oh! Susanna" and "Old Folks at Home." The latter became Florida's state song in 1935.

As America's first professional songwriter, Foster played an important role in the country's emerging sense of national identity. His songs also reflect shifting attitudes toward race during the time, notes Martha Nelson, former park services specialist at the Stephen Foster Folk Culture Center State Park.

"Foster's music represents a critical point in American social history because he wrote for minstrel shows and played into the stereotypes of African Americans," says Nelson.

"But by the 1850s, he became a reformer whose music reflected the progression of thought about slavery." Nelson believes that Foster's songs are embedded in American culture and how we see ourselves as Americans. She cites "Oh! Susanna" as a fun song in the folk tradition. It became the theme song for people who followed the gold rush to California in the mid-nineteenth century.

The songs Foster wrote for minstrel shows began to present blacks in a sympathetic manner, showing them to be as human as their white counterparts. Nelson thinks this understanding may have been due to his friendship with Charles Shirash, an abolitionist who influenced Foster's thinking.

Foster's songwriting took place in an era when copyright laws gave composers limited legal protection for their works. Because of this limitation, he earned far less money than he should have. Worse, perhaps, to pay debts, he relinquished the rights to many of his compositions, thus losing a fortune in potential income for himself and his heirs.

Although Foster wrote close to three hundred songs, his output began to dwindle by the mid-1850s when he was beset by anxiety over mounting debts. His drinking and his financial setbacks ate away at his marriage to his wife, Jane,

Stephen Foster Folk Culture Center State Park.
Photo courtesy of Visit Florida.

for whom he had written the 1854 song "Jeanie with the Light Brown Hair."

By 1864, Foster was living in a hotel room in New York City, poor, sick and alone. As the feverish composer tried to summon the maid, he fell and hit his head against a wash-basin. It was a fatal blow. Foster died at age thirty-seven, penniless except for the thirty-eight cents in his pocket, notes the Foster Hall Collection.

While Foster suffered a miserable end, his songs have established him at the forefront of American folk music. His name lives on at the Stephen Foster Memorial at the University of Pittsburgh, and at the Stephen Foster Folk Culture Center State Park, in White Springs, Florida.

Located beside the Suwannee River, the 880-acre park was built as a memorial to the songwriter. It includes rental cabins, a crafters square, the Stephen Foster Museum, and a two-hundred-foot-high brick carillon tower the park claims as the world's largest tubular bell instrument. An annual Florida Folk Festival is held there each fall to celebrate the state's cultural heritage.

A guide dressed in period costume directs visitors to dioramas that chronicle Stephen Foster's life, one that has become melodically ingrained in American musical history.

Cedar Key Fishermen's Monument

Address: In front of Cedar Key City Hall, 490 Second Street, Cedar Key. (352) 543–5132. Levy County.

In April 2006, the University of Florida Institute of Food and Agriculture Sciences (IFAS) issued a press release making the news official: Cedar Key, a former commercial fishing village on the Gulf of Mexico, had become the state's No. 1 producer of cultured hard clams.

In a maritime variation on the "turning lemons into lemonade" cliché, Cedar Key managed to reinvent itself in the face of hard times, thanks to the resilience and determination of its commercial fishermen.

Those hard times stemmed from an amendment to the Florida Constitution known as the Limiting Marine Net Fishing Amendment or simply as the "net ban." In November 1994, a 72 percent majority of Florida residents voted to make it unlawful for commercial fishermen to use large entangling nets, such as gill nets and trammel nets, in Florida waters. These kinds of nets are effective at capturing certain kinds of fish that had been over-fished in recent years, environmentalists said. Also, the nets were known to inadvertently capture "nontarget" species, such as whales and dolphins.

The amendment, now contained in Article X, Section 16, of the Florida Constitution, permits other types of nets but with restrictions that many commercial fishermen consider unreasonable (Adams et al. 2000).

On September 30, 2003, the *Naples Daily News* published a special report on "The Fight over Fish," examining the effects of the net ban on the Gulf Coast environment and on commercial and recreational fishermen. *Naples Daily News* reporters noted that for recreational fishermen and local environmentalists who were against gillnetting of what they considered over-fished species like mullet, the amendment was good news.

For the commercial fishermen of Cedar Key, however, the amendment meant lost income and the forced cessation of a way of life. For generations, Cedar Key's commercial fisher-

Cedar Key Fishermen's Monument. Photo courtesy of Beth Davis.

men families had used large gill nets to catch mullet. This method was essential to their livelihood. Once the amendment became part of the constitution, however, commercial fishermen had to rely on cast nets in Florida's waters. Such nets cover less area and thus catch fewer fish.

Gill net fishermen who had previously caught as much as five thousand pounds of mullet daily, depending on season, were now likely to catch around one hundred pounds daily with a cast net.

A marine economist was quoted as saying that many people who had voted in favor of the amendment didn't actually know what they were voting for, because they didn't know the real issues behind it.

The *Naples Daily News* also reported that a well-funded lobbying campaign by anti-net forces heavily influenced how voters reacted at the polls in 1994. Promoters of the ban spent $1.4 million to persuade voters that gill nets were harmful to marine life.

With only three hundred thousand dollars in campaign funds, Florida's commercial fishermen may have felt like David standing up to Goliath. Unlike the biblical story, however, the 1994 battle of the net ban was won by the bigger opponent.

Today, more than ten years after the amendment was passed into Florida law, local fishing communities have been radically transformed. Fishing techniques that were passed down for more than a hundred years have passed into oblivion.

Cedar Key resident Beth Davis, whose family has lived and fished on the key for seven generations, says that there are ten-year-old children in her town who have never seen a gill net. As someone whose father, husband and son are all commercial fishermen, she thinks the younger generation's unfamiliarity with their heritage is a sad thing. After all, she notes, the community of Cedar Key was founded on commercial fishing. "Cedar Key has retained that whole commercial fishing atmosphere, and that's what we were afraid of losing," Davis says. "It's part of our heritage and the heritage of Cedar Key."

Many residents of Cedar Key share Davis' sentiments. Back when the amendment passed into law, locals knew that the days of the gillnetting tradition were numbered. Residents wanted the world to know why the village had been the way it was, so they installed a monument to pay tribute to all those hardworking local fishermen who contributed to Cedar Key's heritage.

The brick-and-granite monument reads: "Dedicated to the commercial net fishermen of the community. July 1, 1995." The date represents the day that the net ban took effect.

The monument, about five feet tall, bears the likeness of a fisherman pulling in a net as he stands at the stern of his "bird dog" (boat). Above the fisherman, the sun is setting.

For him, and for an aspect of the fishing industry that's now relegated to Florida history, it is the last sunset.

The net ban has had devastating effects on commercial fishing families in Florida, notes a 1999 family life study conducted by the University of Florida IFAS (Eversole 1999). UF researchers found that among the forty-four couples interviewed at intervals between 1994 and 1998, the sudden economic hardships caused by the net ban had thrown some marriages and families into chaos.

The couples' percentage of family income from fishing dropped from 80 to 55 percent; wives' earnings made a bigger contribution to the families' incomes; wives of full-time fishermen experienced great stress; both husbands and wives reported signs of depression; and the couples' divorce rate rose to four times the state average.

To ease the burdens, Florida offered assistance programs and job retraining to the state's commercial fishermen. That retraining encouraged many Cedar Key fishermen to turn to clam farming. The result? Some people now refer to Cedar Key as "Clamalot."

Indeed, statistics from the U.S. Department of Agriculture (USDA) prove that Florida's clamming industry has entered a golden age. A 1998 Aquaculture Census conducted by the USDA revealed that Florida produces more hard clams by volume than any other state (Woods 2006). About 80 percent of Florida hard clams originate from the state's west coast, with Cedar Key producing 70 percent of the total, the census indicated.

Cedar Key clam farmers lease coastal waters where they farm clams grown in mesh bags, notes Davis. The clams grow in the Gulf of Mexico between the Suwannee River to the north and the Waccasassa River to the south.

As for the Cedar Key Fishermen's Monument, it reminds residents and visitors that generations of local fishermen cast a wide and proud net over Florida's commercial fishing industry.

2

Northeast Florida

Olustee Battlefield Monuments

Address: Olustee Battlefield Historic State Park, U.S. 90, Olustee. (386) 758–0400. Baker County.

Most people don't associate Florida with Civil War battles, but when the five-hour Battle of Olustee was over on February 20, 1864, the blood of more than 1,800 Union casualties and 946 Confederate casualties had turned a northwest Florida pine forest from green to red (Olustee Battlefield Historic State Park).

That February, Union general Truman A. Seymour led about 5,500 soldiers west from Jacksonville in a quest to disrupt Confederate transportation links and to cut off Confederate food supplies.

Confederate brigadier general Joseph Finegan, aware of the Union troop movements, chose an Olustee pine forest bordered by a lake, Ocean Pond, and a swamp as the site for his forces to confront their adversary.

Today that historic confrontation is brought to life at the Olustee Battlefield Historic State Park, in northern Florida. Cannons, monuments, a park ranger and an interpretive center take the visitor on a trip through time to the largest Civil War battle fought in Florida. Both sides came to battle equipped with individual strengths, as noted by Union colonel Joseph Hawley:

> The Confederates knew the ground. . . . The enemy had the great advantage with . . . being on the defensive and ready. . . . The Confederate loss was 940, the Union loss 1,861. . . . It was one of the sideshows of the great war.

Olustee Battlefield Monument.

"Sideshow" or not, the Battle of Olustee stands out in Civil War history for several reasons including the heroism of three African American troops on the Union side. Numbering among the approximately 11,000 total participants were the First North Carolina Colored Infantry, the Eighth U.S. Colored Infantry and the Fifty-fourth Massachusetts Colored Infantry.

The latter had been organized in 1863 by young Robert Gould Shaw, who was appointed colonel of the Fifty-fourth by then-Massachusetts governor John A. Andrew. Shaw died that same year at Battle Wagner on Morris Island, in South Carolina.

The bravery of the Fifty-fourth was captured in the 1989 film *Glory*, costarring actors Morgan Freeman and Denzel Washington as soldiers of the Fifty-fourth and Matthew Broderick as Colonel Shaw.

Soldiers of the Fifty-fourth Massachusetts Colored Infantry marched into battle at Olustee shouting, "Three cheers for Massachusetts and seven dollars a month!" That amount was the difference in pay between white and colored Union infantry, notes the online site battleofolustee.org.

When the Battle of Olustee ended, the score was:

Union killed: 203; Confederates killed: 93.

Union wounded: 1,152; Confederates wounded: 847.

Union missing: 506; Confederate missing: 6.

It was a terrible loss for the Union.

Percentagewise, the battle was one of the bloodiest fought during the Civil War, and, when it was over, both sides combined took almost a thousand prisoners. Including the Seminole Indian Wars, it was the bloodiest battle ever fought in Florida.

Colonel Charles W. Fribley was one of the Union officers killed during the Battle of Olustee. He had been appointed colonel of the Eighth U.S. Colored Infantry four months prior to the battle.

On February 23, three days after the battle, thirty-nine-year-old Brigadier General Seymour, a Vermont native, a graduate of West Point and now commanding officer of the U.S. forces in Florida, sent a letter to Brigadier General Finegan, the Irish-born, Florida-dwelling commanding officer of the Confederate forces.

Seymour's letter requested that Union prisoners captured at Olustee be remanded to the Union side. It also requested that, if found, Colonel Fribley's body be interred in a marked grave so his family could eventually remove his remains for proper burial (Seymour 1864).

General Finegan, who prior to the war had been a planter and a lumberman in Nassau County, Florida, sent a written reply to General Seymour on the following day. Finegan politely advised that the wounded Union prisoners would not be released until a plan was devised by his government regarding the exchange of prisoners. Furthermore, he added, nobody had as yet identified Colonel Fribley's body (Finegan 1864).

So disdainfully did Confederate soldiers look upon a white Union commander of a black regiment that if he were to have been captured, he would more likely have been killed than imprisoned. Afterward, when Confederate brigadier general William Gardner sent some of Fribley's recovered belongings to Fribley's widow, Gardner made it clear that he did so for the sake of her grief and not because of any concern for an officer commanding African American soldiers.

Today Olustee Battlefield Historic State Park is listed on the National Register of Historic Places. In 2003, Olustee Battlefield received the Congressional Black Caucus Veterans' Braintrust Award.

General Colin Powell established the award to honor African American veterans of the Civil War and present-day volunteers who pay tribute to its black regiments, such as those who participate in the annual reenactment in February at Olustee Battlefield.

A cannon rests in front of the monument to the Battle of Olustee. The gray monument stands tall on the former battlefield. Erected in 1912, it bears the brunt of the ages, but its words vividly conjure the memory of those who fell there:

> The Battle of Olustee was fought on this ground, February 20, 1864, between 5,000 Confederate troops commanded by Gen. Joseph E. Finegan, and 6,000 Federal troops under Gen. Truman Seymour. The Federals were defeated with a loss of 2,000 men. Confederate loss was less than 1,000.

The back of the monument is inscribed:

> To the men who fought and triumphed here in defense of their homes and firesides, this monument is erected by the United Daughters of the Confederacy, aided by the State of Florida in commemoration to their devotion to the cause of liberty and states' sovereignty.

Next to this monument rests a headstone-shaped monument placed by the United Daughters of the Confederacy, Florida Division. It is inscribed:

> In memory of Brig. Gen. Joseph Finegan, Commander of District of Middle and East Florida. So well did he perform his part that a signal victory over the Federals was won in the Battle of Olustee February 20, 1864.

Fernandina Beach Shrimping Monument

Address: Centre Street, overlooking the Amelia River in Fernandina Beach, on Amelia Island. (904) 261–7378. Nassau County.

At the foot of Centre Street on the northwest corner of Amelia Island, a tall, slim monument pays tribute to the shrimping industry in Fernandina Beach.

A polished granite pylon capped by a copper shrimp boat, the monument was constructed at the Fernandina Beach docks by the Coastal Monument Company.

The monument, which is not inscribed, commemorates Fernandina as the birthplace of the modern shrimping industry. (The town of Fernandina did not become Fernandina Beach until 1951.)

For many years, local resident Robert Lannon promoted the idea of erecting such a monument. He was a former shrimper who worked local waters and who had spent long periods shrimping along the coasts of Texas and South America.

Lannon's dream became a reality through major funding from the Shrimp Festival Committee of Fernandina Beach. The monument was dedicated on May 2, 1991.

Admirers of the monument can learn more about shrimp fishing in Florida at the nearby Amelia Island Museum of History. Interpretive panels, photographs and artifacts chronicle the development and progress of Fernandina Beach and provide an overview of the area's shrimping industry.

Today 80 percent of Florida's Atlantic white shrimp come from the waters offshore Amelia Island. These waters are abundant with white and brown shrimp.

In the 1800s, local shrimpers routinely rowed their boats to inshore waters to cast their nets. Around 1900, shrimper Solicito "Mike" Salvador, who had come from his native Sicily to Fernandina Beach, ventured farther.

He steered his boat into offshore waters and returned with a bounty of shrimp far greater than those netted by less adventurous shrimpers. Salvador wrote about his magnificent catches to friends and family in Sicily. Inspired by his success, they migrated to Fernandina Beach to become shrimpers.

By 1913, shrimping had become a major industry in Fernandina, thanks to the technical innovations of Salvador and other fishermen who came there from Italy, Greece, Portugal, Scandinavia and elsewhere.

Captain Billy Corkum, formerly of Massachusetts, modified his trawl net, as did Salvatore Tringali, a native of Sicily who added weights to his net. These improvements enabled them to increase their catch.

Another net-maker whose efforts boosted the local shrimping industry was William Billy Burbank, a shrimper and fisherman from Cumberland Island who moved to Amelia Island in 1915. The nets that Burbank designed created a demand among local shrimpers, and soon Burbank's net-making business became a successful enterprise.

Boat builders and chandlers arrived on Amelia Island, and area shrimpers graduated from sailboats and rowboats to motorboats that could maneuver deeper waters.

In the 1920s, Fernandina was crowned the shrimping capital of the world. Today, an elegant monument reminds visitors that the modern shrimping industry was born and prospered on these very shores.

Shrimping
Monument.

Fort Caroline National Memorial

Address: 12713 Fort Caroline Road, 13 miles east of downtown Jacksonville, in Jacksonville. (904) 641–7155. http://www.nps. gov/foca. Duval County.

In the sixteenth century, French Protestants known as Huguenots were a persecuted minority in Catholic France.

In 1562, French mariner Jean Ribault led five ships on an expedition to the New World to find a suitable site for a Huguenot colony of refuge. On May 1, he landed in northern Florida and reached the mouth of the St. Johns River, which he named Rivière de Mai (River of May).

Ribault made port on an island he called Mayport, notes the National Park Service's web page about Fort Caroline. There he built a column with a bronze shield representing the coat of arms of Queen Catherine de Médicis, the mother of France's King Charles IX. Ribault claimed the land for France.

As time would reveal, this was not one of Ribault's better ideas. Spanish explorer Juan Ponce de León had already claimed Florida for Spain in 1513 when, according to legend, he arrived in search of the Fountain of Youth. Ribault did not remain in Florida. He headed north to the Carolinas and eventually sailed back to France.

In 1564, René Goulaine de Laudonnière, who had accompanied Ribault on his first journey, led a follow-up expedition to Florida and established a French colony on a bluff along the Rivière de Mai/St. Johns River, a few miles north of Mayport. Laudonnière named the colony la Caroline in honor of Charles IX and erected a triangular-shaped fort.

The French settlement was doomed to fail. Fort Caroline was inadequately prepared for enemy attacks, and the colonists had a hard time planting crops.

Initially the colonists had been on good terms with the native Timucuans, who shared their food with the French. A clash of cultures eventually gnawed at the friendly relationship, and in a short time, the colonists were nearing starvation. They were saved only by the arrival of Jean

Ribault Monument, Fort Caroline National Memorial.

Ribault, who returned to la Caroline with shiploads of food and supplies. He also brought more colonists.

The French attempt at a permanent colony in Florida was a reckless and ill-fated one. When King Phillip II of Spain learned of la Caroline's existence, he was not about to look away.

King Phillip sent Admiral Pedro Menéndez de Avilés to rid Florida of the French encroachers. In September 1565, Menéndez and his fleet arrived at what we know today as St. Augustine, south of la Caroline, and made encampment there.

Intending to attack the Spanish, Ribault and some of his men sailed south toward Menéndez's camp; however, his timing was poor. This was September, which, as Floridians know, is the height of the hurricane season. A hurricane whipped up and caught Ribault's ships in its ferocious winds, running them aground.

Menéndez and five hundred soldiers marched to the poorly defended Fort Caroline, where the Spanish killed about 140 French colonists. Mercy was shown only to some women and children. Laudonnière and about fifty colonists managed to escape and sail to France.

After his victory at Fort Caroline, Menéndez headed back to his encampment. He captured Ribault's party at a place that became known as Matanzas, the Spanish word for "slaughter." There he butchered Ribault and all of his followers except those who declared, perhaps desperately, that they were Catholics.

Once firmly under Spanish rule, the fort at la Caroline became known as San Mateo. In 1568, French forces attacked the fort and burned it to the ground.

Today the Fort Caroline National Memorial preserves the history of the first attempted permanent French colony in the United States.

The National Park Service built a partial fort that is an interpretation of the original fort. Visitors learn about Fort Caroline from the park rangers.

A wayside near the arched entrance to the fort quotes these words of French carpenter Nicholas LeChalleux, who escaped Menéndez's attack on the French colony in 1565:

> The Spaniards made a horrible tragic slaughter of our forces, so great was the anger and hatred they had for our nation. They vied with one another to see who could best cut the throats of our people.

The column that Ribault erected in 1562 no longer exists, but there is a replica monument at Fort Caroline National Memorial. It too bears a bronze shield representing Catherine de Médicis' coat of arms.

The monument is inscribed:

> Erected by the Florida Daughters of the American Revolution, May 1, 1924, commemorating the first landing of Protestants on American soil. This is a replica of a marker placed on or near this spot by Jean Ribault, May 1, 1562, taking possession of Florida for France.

Camp Blanding Memorial Park

Address: 5629 S.R. 16, 8 miles east of U.S. 301, Starke. (904) 682–3196. Clay County.

"When people visit Camp Blanding, they're struck by two things: how big it is and how significant it is," says Major Greg Parsons, curator of Camp Blanding Museum, in Starke.

Camp Blanding is named for Lieutenant General Albert H. Blanding, an 1894 graduate of what is now the University of Florida and a founder of the Florida National Guard. He commanded the Fifty-third Brigade, Twenty-seventh Division, during World War I and the Thirty-first Infantry Division until 1940, the same year he retired as chief of the National Guard Bureau, notes GlobalSecurity.org.

During World War II, Camp Blanding was a major U.S. Army training center. Troops trained at the camp encompass nine U.S. infantry divisions, five infantry regiments (including the 508th Parachute Infantry), three tank destroyer battalions, the Seventy-fourth Field Artillery Brigade, two field artillery groups and three field artillery regiments, as recorded by the Florida Department of Military Affairs, Florida National Guard.

If you have seen the movies *The Longest Day* and *Saving Private Ryan*, you will recall scenes of American paratroopers and soldiers landing on Normandy's beaches. In real life, these servicemen trained at Camp Blanding. The 1997 film *G.I. Jane*, starring actress Demi Moore, was partially filmed at the camp.

Today Camp Blanding is a Florida National Guard Military Reservation. The military installation encompasses about 73,000 square acres.

The history of Camp Blanding and the soldiers who trained there comes alive through documents and artifacts displayed in the Camp Blanding Museum, which is located in a World War II-era military barracks that is presently operated by the Florida National Guard.

The monuments and memorials surrounding Camp Blanding honor the bravery and the selflessness of all the

Florida Regimental Memorial, Camp Blanding Memorial Park.

trainees, regardless of whether they hailed from Florida. These memorials share park space with World War II–era vehicles such as the M4 Sherman, the main American tank used during the war, and the Douglas C-47 Skytrain, a form of aerial military transport.

The Florida Regimental Memorial was dedicated in 1990 to the memory of the Florida National Guardsmen who served in World War II in the Pacific and European theaters of operations.

Large bronze plaques on the walls of the memorial pay tribute to the 106th Engineers, Medical and Quartermasters; the 265th Coast Artillery; the 116th Field Artillery; and the 124th Infantry.

In front of the memorial stands a nearly life-size bronze statue called the "Soldiers' Monument." Created by sculptor Enzo Torcoletti of St. Augustine, the statue stands on a 3' × 6' × 4' base.

The statue depicts a soldier looking upward, a weapon in his right hand. His left arm is raised to the sky. The statue is representative of, and dedicated to, the GI who served and trained at Camp Blanding.

The granite base of the statue is inscribed:

May each of us now fight as diligently for lasting peace as we did in prosecuting this war.
Joseph C. Hutchinson, Brig. Gen., USA.

Not only does Camp Blanding Memorial Park contain a memorial to an anonymous soldier. It also features a number of monuments to individual infantry divisions and regiments.

Camp Blanding was the birthplace of the Sixty-third Infantry Division and therefore is a proper setting for a monument to the more than nine thousand battle casualties suffered by the division during World War II, notes the Sixty-third Infantry Division Association.

The Sixty-third Infantry was activated at Camp Blanding in June 1943 and de-activated in September 1945. Known as the "Blood and Fire Sixty-third," its emblem is a bloodied, golden sword set against a crimson flame. The monument bears the emblem and is inscribed:

> 63rd Infantry Division.
> Ardennes—Alsace
> Rhineland
> Central Europe.
> Battle casualties 8019. [*That number has since increased.*]
> Blood and Fire.

The monument to the officers and men who served with the 508th Parachute Infantry Regiment is really a history carved in stone, as evidenced by its inscription:

> Wheresoever dispersed, activated at Camp Blanding, Florida 28 October 1942. They were later attached to the 82nd Airborne Division and participated in the parachute assaults into Normandy on 6 June 1944 and into Holland on 17 September 1944.
>
> They fought in the Ardennes in December 1944 and in the Rhineland in May 1945. On V-E Day they were chosen as the Honor Guard for Supreme Headquarters, Allied Expeditionary Forces. Four years, one month and four days after they came into existence, they passed onto history at Camp Kilmer, N.J., on 24 November 1946.

There are several granite monuments to individuals at Camp Blanding Memorial Park, but one in particular stands out because of the extraordinary actions of the man to whom it is dedicated: First Sergeant Leonard Funk, Jr.

Funk trained at Camp Blanding and served with Com-

Monuments to 508th Parachute Infantry Regiment, William "Woody" Braswell and others, Camp Blanding Memorial Park.

pany C, 508th Parachute Infantry. On January 29, 1945, he received the Congressional Medal of Honor for his bravery. Camp Blanding Museum tells the story:

Funk and his unit captured eighty enemy Germans in Holzheim, Belgium, on January 29, 1945. Funk returned to the fight, leaving only four soldiers to guard the German prisoners. While he was gone, German soldiers captured the American guards and freed the prisoners. Not knowing that this event was unfolding, Funk happened to walk into their path.

A German officer shoved a pistol into Funk's stomach and demanded that Funk and his men surrender. Pretending to acquiesce, Funk unslung his Thompson submachine gun and rapidly riddled the officer. The four captured Americans sprung into action and helped Funk kill twenty-one German soldiers and wound another twenty-four. The rest were taken captive.

Funk's monument cites him as "outstanding leader, magnificent soldier, cherished friend." The list of honors and awards given to Funk by France, the Netherlands and the United States is so long that it covers the entire face of the monument.

Another monument dedicated to a brave individual is that of William "Woody" Braswell of Company G, 124th Infantry Regiment, Florida National Guard, Company B, Nineteenth Infantry Regiment, Twenty-fourth Infantry Division.

Braswell was one of the most decorated Florida Guardsman. He was awarded the Distinguished Service Cross, the Silver Star and two Purple Hearts for his service in the Philippines during World War II.

Another Camp Blanding monument, etched with the likenesses of women of all races who served in the Armed Forces, features a lighted torch and the words, "in memory of those brave service women who held high the torch of liberty."

The Hero Monument was erected by citizens of Clay County to America's military heroes, historic and contemporary. The Great Seal of the United States decorates the top of the granite monument. Beneath the seal, the monument's long granite wall is inscribed, "Dedicated to our heroes, all who serve."

Etched into the face of the monument are two crossed American flags flanked by emblems of the U.S. Army, the U.S. Navy, the U.S. Air Force, the U.S. Merchant Marines, the U.S. Marines and the National Guard. Below, the monument reads simply: "WWI, WWII, Korea, Vietnam, Desert Storm."

Another section of Camp Blanding Memorial Park, the "Walk Through Time" exhibit, is devoted to black Floridians with military connections. A vertical, black granite monument stands in front of interpretive signs that relay the historical contributions of Florida's black soldiers. The monument reads:

> Military service of black Floridians 1565–1997. Little known or appreciated is the fact that persons of African origin or heritage have served the military needs of Florida for more than four hundred years.

Monument to Women in U.S. Armed Forces, Camp Blanding Memorial Park.

Black Floridians Monument, Camp Blanding Memorial Park.

Men and women of African heritage have been an important and essential part of Florida's military history under the Spanish, British, American and even the Confederate military forces.

Their service has been a long, unusual and important part of our state's military heritage, and it is time for their contribution to receive its proper and appropriate recognition.

It is to that purpose that this permanent "Walk Through Time" exhibit is dedicated in recognition of the services of those Americans of African descent.

These and other monuments and exhibits at Camp Blanding Memorial Park serve important functions for current and retired military personnel and their families, as well as for everyday visitors. The park holds a special importance for members of the "Greatest Generation," as Tom Brokaw called it. Frank Towers, a board member of Camp Blanding Museum who trained at Camp Blanding during World War II, describes the memorial site as a place of reminiscence for the men who trained there and for the people who lived through the war.

Additionally, Towers notes, "for generations who weren't born before World War II, the museum and memorial park educate them about the worldwide significance of World War II and its impact on our country and the freedoms we enjoy today."

Towers served in the Thirtieth Infantry Division, which trained at Camp Blanding between October 1942 and May 1943. He notes that Thirtieth had a reputation as the No. 1 infantry division in the European theater of operations, so the granite monument has special significance for him.

These words appear on the monument:

> Normandy, Northern France, Rhineland, Ardennes-Alsace, Central Europe. Workhorse of the Western Front.

Many Camp Blanding trainees who served in various wars received the Purple Heart and the Congressional Medal of Honor. The camp's Purple Heart Memorial is inscribed:

> Awarded for wounds or death as result of an act of an opposing armed force. Dedicated to all those who shed their life's blood in the cause of freedom. Erected by Rotary Club of Starke, Fla.

The Medal of Honor Monument is the centerpiece of the park and is its tallest monument. In fact, no monument can exceed it in height. It is dedicated to the thirty-six Medal of Honor recipients who trained here with their respective divisions.

Every day, the United States loses more and more World War II veterans. Fortunately, Camp Blanding Museum and Memorial Park keep alive many of their stories so current and future generations who visit the site will understand something basic.

For a tumultuous period of time around the world, thousands of men trained here to keep America a land of the free. By doing so, they made Camp Blanding the home of the brave.

Medal of Honor Monument, Camp Blanding Memorial Park.

Albert A. Murphree Memorial

Address: University of Florida campus, the courtyard in front of Peabody Hall. Gainesville. (352) 392–3261. Alachua County.

In Greek mythology, Prometheus was a benefactor to humankind. According to legend, the Titan not only stole fire from the gods and gave it to mortals, but he also taught them arts and sciences.

If you have visited Rockefeller Center in New York City, you may have seen the famous gilded bronze sculpture *Prometheus*, which was sculpted by Art Deco artist Paul Manship.

Thousands of students and visitors who walk the University of Florida campus are unaware that there is a connection between the Prometheus sculpture and the bronze statue that sits between Peabody Hall and Library East in the campus' historic district.

In 1946, Manship sculpted the fifteen-foot-tall bronze statue of Dr. Albert A. Murphree, the university's second president. In so doing, he sculpted the likeness of a man who, like Prometheus, was a teacher and a benefactor to mankind.

The UF sculpture depicts a robed Murphree seated on a chair, his left hand clutching a book, the open palm of his right hand extended upward, as though he is teaching to his students.

The base of the statue is inscribed:

> With kindness, vision and wisdom he devoted his life to the cause of education, and as president 1909–1927 he laid the foundation upon which this university is built.
>
> Erected in grateful memory by the people of Florida. MCMXLVI.

According to the *University of Florida News*, Murphree was born in Alabama in 1870. He earned a Bachelor of Arts degree from the University of Nashville in 1894 and taught mathematics at various high schools and colleges in the South.

In 1895, Murphree became a mathematics instructor at West Florida Seminary, in Tallahassee, and became its presi-

Albert A. Murphree Memorial. Photo courtesy of Ray Carson, University of Florida News Bureau.

dent in 1897. That same year, he married Jennie Henderson, the daughter of one of the seminary's trustees. In 1901, the seminary became Florida State College.

In 1905, the Florida legislature formed a new state university in Gainesville. Andrew Sledd had been president of the University of Florida at Lake City but was tapped to become the first president of the University of Florida in Gainesville.

Murphree, meanwhile, was serving as first president of the Florida State College for Women. In 1909, he took over Sledd's role at the University of Florida.

In this new position, Murphree wasted no time making changes. He reorganized the university, introducing four academic colleges: the College of Arts and Sciences, the College of Law, the College of Agriculture and the College of Engineering.

Under Murphree's leadership, enrollment grew and the university expanded. During his eighteen-year presidency, the Graduate School, a School of Pharmacy, a Teacher's College, a School of Architecture and a College of Commerce and Journalism were established.

Murphree died in his sleep in 1927 at the age of fifty-seven. The vice president assumed temporary leadership until the following year, when John J. Tigert became president.

Murphree Hall, a women's dormitory at Florida State University, is named for Murphree's wife Jennie.

Dr. Austin Cary Memorial and Memorial Forest

Address: 10625 NE Waldo Road, Gainesville. (352) 371–8041. Alachua County.

Since 1936, the University of Florida has owned forest land on S.R. 24 between Gainesville and Waldo. The university's School of Forest Resources and Conservation manages the forest.

Although the 2,080-acre forest is not accessible to the public, people are permitted to commune with nature or to enjoy a secluded picnic lunch in a small area inside the forest's main gate. The centerpiece of this area is the Dr. Austin Cary Memorial.

A bronze plaque on a granite boulder bears this inscription:

> Dr. Austin Cary.
> 1865–1936.
> The Society of American Foresters and Friends of Dr. Austin Cary have erected this memorial in deep appreciation of his unending interest and effort toward the promotion of sound forestry practices in the United States.

Austin Cary was born in Maine in 1865. He graduated from Bowdoin College in 1887 and continued his studies at Princeton and John Hopkins. Some of Cary's family members were lumberman, so it seemed natural for him to pursue a career in forestry.

In 1898, he took a job with a lumber company in Maine, thus becoming the first forester to work for an American forest products industry, notes the Florida Society of American Foresters, which inducted Cary to its Hall of Fame in 2003.

During his career, Dr. Cary contributed articles to forestry journals, lectured at Harvard University and taught at the Yale School of Forestry.

His nationwide studies of forests, the landmark publication of his *Manual of Northern Woodsman* (1909), his eventual position as logging engineer for the U.S. Forest Service and his knowledge of the forestry industry earned him a fellowship in the Society of American Foresters.

Dr. Austin Cary Memorial and Memorial Park.

While visiting the University of Florida campus in 1936, Cary suffered a fatal heart attack. He was buried in Lake City.

The Southeastern Section of the Society of American Foresters decided to create a memorial to Dr. Cary. The memorial was dedicated in 1939. In further tribute, the University of Florida School of Forest Resources and Conservation named the forest Dr. Austin Cary Memorial Forest.

According to Forest Manager Dan Schultz, the Austin Cary Memorial Forest serves as a large outdoor classroom where students conduct experiments and research and learn about forest protection and management.

This research and experimentation includes studying wood preservation, planting cuttings to different densities, analyzing composted garbage, performing prescribed burnings, and studying different species of slash pine.

The forest is comprised of wetlands, natural stands and loblolly and longleaf pines that are natural to the forest, as well as some sand pine planted for experimental purposes.

Because Cary was seventy-one years old when he died, there were originally seventy-one pine trees planted around his memorial. Unfortunately, some of the young trees did not survive.

Castillo de San Marcos National Monument

Address: 1 S. Castillo Drive, St. Augustine. (904) 829–6506. St. Johns County.

Within 144 city blocks bursting with buildings listed on the National Register of Historic Places, St. Augustine's most recognized attraction is the Castillo de San Marcos National Monument. Set on more than twenty acres overlooking the Matanzas River, the imposing stone structure is the oldest existing masonry fort in the continental United States.

The Old City of St. Augustine is the oldest permanent European colony in America. Settled by the Spanish in 1565, forty-two years prior to the Jamestown settlement in Virginia, St. Augustine was vulnerable to attack from enemy invaders. Sir Francis Drake burned the city to the ground in 1668, prompting the Spanish to build a series of nine wooden forts.

Today, thanks to guided tours of Castillo de San Marcos led by National Park Service rangers, visitors learn that the fort was meant to protect St. Augustine's harbor, the town itself and the Spanish treasure fleets sailing past Florida's shores. However, after fires and natural wood rot destroyed each successive fort, the Spanish Crown agreed to finance the construction of a superior fortress of stone.

In 1672, nearly one hundred years after the founding of St. Augustine, the Spanish broke ground on the Castillo de San Marcos ("St. Mark's Castle"). Park rangers note that the huge masonry fortress was built with a form of concrete made of sand and *coquina*, soft limestone made of crushed oyster shells. The fort's thirty-six-foot-high walls, its diamond-shaped bastions, its living quarters, moat and seawall were completed in 1695, according to Jeff Jones, a park ranger at the fort (The walls were expanded to thirty-three feet by 1756).

Total building costs were the equivalent of $218,633. The fortification site comprises 20½ acres.

Castillo de San Marcos was so impenetrable that in 1702, when British forces commanded by General James Moore attacked and burned the town, the fort remained unharmed.

Fort at Castillo de San Marcos National Monument.

The same held true when British general James Ogle-thorpe, founder of the colony of Georgia, led an unsuccess-ful attack on St. Augustine in 1740.

Enemies trying to gain access to the fort would run into the expected cannon fire as well as a painful surprise: yucca. The Spanish planted yucca around and on top of the walls of their forts for a defensive reason: The plant grows in clusters of long, sharp sword-shaped leaves.

In 1763, Spain ceded the colony of Florida to Great Britain. Twenty years later, Florida reverted to Spanish control.

In 1821, Spain ceded Florida to the United States. Four years later, Castillo de San Marcos was renamed Fort Marion. During the Second Seminole War (1835–42), Fort Marion was used as a prison for captured Native Americans. During the Spanish-American War, it served as a military prison.

In 1924, the fort was designated a National Monument. In 1942, it again became known as Castillo de San Marcos.

In addition to the Spanish, British and U.S. Territorial flags, the Confederate flag also flew over Castillo de San Marcos. It was occupied for less than one year by the Confederacy.

Here are some of the highlights you'll see when you tour the fort:

The powder magazine (storage); the chapel; the British Room, used for storing supplies and sleeping; storage rooms that were stockpiled with foods; the guardrooms where rotating guards slept and ate; the diamond-shaped bastions of saints Augustine, Peter, Paul and Charles; and "la necessaria," the original bathrooms.

Castillo de San Marcos has survived five centuries. While its cannons no longer roar and its soldiers no longer drill in the Plaza de Armas (courtyard), the fort's powerful, enduring presence gives testimony to Spain's importance and influence in Florida's history.

Henry Flagler Memorial

Address: In front of Flagler College, King and Cordova streets, St. Augustine. St. Johns County.

Nearly everyone has heard of John D. Rockefeller, but few people outside of Florida have heard of Henry Flagler. That's ironic, considering Flagler was Rockefeller's partner in Standard Oil.

Moreover, from an architectural and developmental standpoint, Henry Flagler left a larger, more enduring footprint on Florida's east coast than did perhaps anyone else.

Whitehall, Flagler's Palm Beach mansion, is now the Flagler Museum. Here, tour guides lay out Flagler's life and the history of Whitehall. He was a shrewd businessman who became one of the nation's wealthiest hotel and railroad barons.

Henry Morrison Flagler was born in 1830 in Hopewell, New York, the museum notes. He worked as a clerk and salesman, started his own business and, after the Civil War, formed a partnership with John D. Rockefeller in an oil refining company, Standard Oil.

Flagler and his first wife, Mary Harkness Flagler, visited northern Florida in 1878 in the hope that the mild climate would improve her poor health, but Mary died in 1881. Two years later, Flagler married Mary's former nurse, Ida Alice Shourds. They honeymooned in St. Augustine.

It was there that Flagler built his first hotel, the Ponce de Leon, now Flagler College. He built and bought more hotels in St. Augustine: the Casa Monica and the Alcazar, which is across the street from Flagler College. The Alcazar is now the Lightner Museum.

In Palm Beach, Flagler built the Royal Poinciana Hotel. In the 1890s, it was considered one of the world's largest wooden structures. The Breakers, a Palm Beach resort hotel that overlooks the Atlantic Ocean, remains his hotel masterpiece.

Originally called the Palm Beach Inn, the first Breakers burned in a fire in 1903, the hotel's history notes. Likewise, the second Breakers burned down in 1925, supposedly due to a guest's overheated curling iron.

The magnificent architectural details of the current Breakers, built soon after, include twin towers emulating the towers of the Villa Medici in Rome and an entrance fountain resembling that in Florence's Boboli Gardens. Flagler's lavish hotels enticed society's elite to winter in Florida.

If the third time was a charm for Flagler's Breakers, it also was for his marriage. Second wife Ida Alice Shourds Flagler suffered from delusions and other mental problems, which forced Flagler to institutionalize her in 1895.

Henry Flagler Memorial, Henry Flagler College.

In 1901, new laws in Florida that made "incurable insanity" grounds for divorce enabled Flagler to sever his marital ties to Ida Alice and marry Mary Lily Kenan. He was 71. She was 34. As a wedding present to her, Flagler built Whitehall, a fifty-five-room, sixty-thousand-square-foot Beaux Arts mansion overlooking the Intracoastal Waterway.

Touted as "the Taj Mahal of North America," the Gilded Age mansion was designed by John Carrere and Thomas Hastings, the same firm that had designed Flager's Hotel Ponce de Leon and the New York Public Library.

Flagler bought the Jacksonville, St. Augustine and Halifax Railroad, which eventually became his Florida East Coast Railway. He extended his railway to Fort Dallas, which we know today as the city of Miami.

Flagler wanted to connect mainland Florida with the Florida Keys and so he spent seven years building his Overseas Railroad (Key West Extension), the culmination of his East Coast Railway.

The extension's track stretched more than one hundred miles out into open water. Its bridges and viaducts connecting the islands of the Florida Keys, including a seven-mile-long bridge at Marathon in the middle keys, were regarded as engineering marvels, notes the Flagler Museum.

The Overseas Railroad was completed in early January of 1912. That month, arriving on the first train to pull into Key West was none other than the baron himself, eighty-two-year-old Henry Flagler. The following year, he fell down a staircase at Whitehall and died.

In Florida, a county, a beach, and various schools, hotels and streets pay tribute to his name. St. Augustine, Miami and Key West, three Florida cities that benefited from Flagler's ambition and achievements, honor him with a memorial statue each.

St. Augustine's statue to Flagler stands at the main entrance to Flagler College. Nearly eight feet tall, the bronze statue shows the railroad baron dressed in a long coat with his right hand tucked in a trouser pocket.

Commissioned by Flagler's third wife, the statue was dedicated in 1916 and is inscribed: "Henry M. Flagler. Born January 2, 1830. Died May 20, 1913."

A nearby tablet reads:

In recognition of the achievements of railroad develop-
ment in the state of Florida and its Overseas Extension to
Key West, this tablet is dedicated to the memory of Henry
M. Flagler, the builder of the Florida East Coast Railway.
Erected by the National Railway Historical Society February
23, 1959 . . .

In 2006, a reproduction of the original statue was un-
veiled at the Key West Bight Ferry Terminal, across from
the former passenger depot of Flagler's Extension.

The statue was commissioned by the Flagler Museum,
which dedicated it to Flagler's vision, determination and
contributions to the state of Florida.

Another reproduction was dedicated in July 2006 to coincide with the 110th anniversary of the incorporation of the
city of Miami.

The statue, donated to Miami-Dade County by Colonel
G. F. Robert Hanke, Flagler's great-grandson, stands outside
the Miami-Dade County Courthouse at 73 W. Flagler Street.

At the dedication of the original statue in St. Augustine
in 1916, then-mayor J. E. Ingraham summed up Flagler's
importance to Florida:

Henry Flagler's faith in Florida was absolute. When other
men hesitated, he went calmly, quietly but persistently along
the way he had chosen, regardless of the criticism of men
who dared to criticize, but who did not dare to do. . . .

(Flagler) Memorial Presbyterian Church

Address: 32 Sevilla Street, St. Augustine. (904) 829–6451. St. Johns County.

Jennie Louise Flagler Benedict was buried holding her infant daughter Margery. They died in 1889.

That year, Jennie's father, the railroad pioneer Henry Flagler, built a church for the St. Augustine community. After Jennie's death, the congregation dedicated the church in memory of Jennie. It was dedicated as Flagler Memorial Presbyterian Church almost one year after her death.

Take a tour of the church. It is the most effective way to learn about Jennie and to appreciate the church's beauty.

Jennie was born in 1855 to Henry Flagler and his first wife, Mary. Jennie married Frederick Benedict and became pregnant; however, Jennie experienced complications while giving birth, and her baby Margery died after only a few hours. Deathly ill herself, Jennie was taken by boat to Florida, where the warmer weather would supposedly mend her, but she perished at sea. Jennie was only thirty-four years old.

The church that memorializes that young woman is among St. Augustine's architectural masterpieces. Designed by the renowned team of Carrere and Hastings, Flagler Memorial Presbyterian Church resembles grand building of the Venetian Renaissance, crowned with a copper dome that ascends 150 feet. Italian artists embellished the poured-concrete church with stunning terracotta frieze work.

The interior of the church featured hand-carved Santo Domingo mahogany woodwork and floors made of Siena marble. The original pipe organ was a three-manual Roosevelt pipe organ.

A wrought-iron gate distinguished by the letter "F" protects the Flagler family mausoleum, which is adjacent to the southwest corner of the church.

It is here that Henry Flagler was laid to rest alongside his first wife Mary, his daughter Jennie and the baby Margery, who was placed in Jennie's arms for eternity.

(Flagler) Memorial Presbyterian Church.

Explore this stunning house of worship and you will marvel at the architectural details that Henry Flagler incorporated into its design. You also will be touched by the story of a church that became a loving tribute to a young woman.

Fort Matanzas National Monument

Address: Visitor Center located 14 miles south of St. Augustine on S.R. A1A, Anastasia Island, St. Augustine. (904) 471–0116. St. Johns County.

When the Spanish settled St. Augustine in 1565, they built a series of forts to defend the city from enemy attack, but after a British invasion in 1740, they realized that enemies could penetrate the city by entering via Matanzas Inlet fourteen miles to the south.

The Spanish had built a wooden watchtower at Matanzas Inlet in 1569, but the 1740 attack convinced the Spanish that they needed a bigger, more durable structure. That same year, they began building Fort Matanzas, a *coquina* fort at the southern entrance to St. Augustine Harbor, on Rattlesnake Island.

Fort Matanzas was completed in 1742 and was accessible only by boat. It had a thirty-foot tower and sat on about two acres of dry ground. The gun deck held five 6–ton cannons, notes the National Park Service.

Fort Matanzas derives its name from the fort's proximity to Matanzas Inlet, where in 1565 St. Augustine's founder Pedro Menéndez de Avilés and his soldiers slaughtered 245 French Huguenots. Matanzas is the Spanish word for "slaughter" or "massacre."

Once completed, the fort was manned by an officer and about ten soldiers on one-month rotating shifts. The number of soldiers assigned to the fort increased fivefold during battle conditions.

Due to the fort's island location, soldiers had no fresh water, so they depended on rainwater collected in a cistern. For provisions, they relied on a monthly supply boat.

Fort Matanzas was abandoned in 1821 when Florida became a U.S. territory. In 1924, it was designated a National Monument. Today it is operated by the National Park Service, which offers guided tours of the fort's history.

Many visitors to the Old City of St. Augustine don't realize that only fourteen miles to the south lies Fort Matanzas

Fort Matanzas National Monument.

National Monument, which is linked to the city's centuries-old military history and is open to tourists.

In 1937, as part of President Franklin D. Roosevelt's Works Project Administration (WPA) program, a *coquina* visitor center was built along A1A on Anastasia Island.

From there, you can take a free ferry ride to the fort. The ride is short, and the waters ripple with wildlife. In the distance, the stone fort, with its low, square walls and rising tower, seems gigantic, but it actually is a compact structure.

The small fort lacks the grandeur of nearby Castillo de San Marcos, but for nearly seventy years it met its primary purpose: to enable soldiers to watch for approaching enemy ships.

There have been restorations and improvements to the fort, including the addition of stairs to replace the pull-up ladder the Spanish soldiers used to gain entry.

Before you visit Fort Matanzas National Monument, call the visitor center to make certain the ferry will be operating.

Gamble Rogers Memorial State Recreation Area

Address: 3100 S. A1A, Flagler Beach. (386) 517–2086. Flagler County.

A stone monument overlooking the Atlantic Ocean stands along the beach at Gamble Rogers Memorial State Recreation Area at Flagler Beach. The inscription reads:

> Gamble Rogers, Florida troubadour, beloved guitarist, storyteller, gentleman. He delighted audiences across the country with his southern Gothic tall tales and intricate guitar style and through his example inspired high aspirations, personal dignity and respect for Florida and humanity. Drowned off this beach, trying to rescue a swimmer in distress, October 10, 1991.

Among those who were fortunate to have known Gamble Rogers well is Charles Steadham, the musician's friend, agent and manager from 1975 to 1991. This is Steadham's fond and wistful recollection of a Florida folk legend:

On the day that Rogers died, Rogers and his wife Nancy were camping at what was then Flagler Beach State Recreation Area. They heard screams for help from the daughter of a Canadian tourist who was drowning in a riptide.

At the time, as a result of severe arthritis in his spine, Rogers could turn his head only by twisting his entire body. Despite this affliction, the musician quickly grabbed an air mattress from under his sleeping bag and dove into the ten-foot-high waves.

Rogers struggled to maintain his hold on the mattress, but the rough seas snatched it from his hands. He couldn't fight the water.

The Canadian tourist drowned. So did Rogers. Steadham believes that Rogers' selfless act was typical of the man.

"He was a consummate Southern gentleman, as honorable and noble a man as you could ever know," Steadham says.

In 1991, the International Kiwanis Foundation posthumously awarded Gamble Rogers with the Robert P. Connelly Medal for Heroism. The award is named for a Kiwanis

Gamble Rogers Memorial State Recreation Area.

member who died while trying to save another person's life. The award reads:

> Gamble Rogers, who lost his life to save the life of another in October, 1991; performing service above and beyond the call of duty . . . Presented by the Kiwanis International Foundation.

James Gamble Rogers IV was born in Winter Park, Florida, on January 31, 1937. He came from a family of renowned architects, a career he intended to follow.

It was the 1960s, and he was on his way to interview for a job with an architectural firm in Cambridge, Massachusetts, when he learned that the popular folk group Serendipity Singers was auditioning for a new member.

Since his teens, the tall and lanky Rogers had been playing guitar and writing and singing songs. He auditioned for the Serendipity Singers and was hired. No doubt, they were impressed by his storytelling abilities as well as his musical prowess.

"Gamble had a mind-boggling command of the King's English," Steadham recalls. "Writers loved to listen to his stories because he had a way with words."

Later, as a solo artist, Rogers earned a reputation as a modern-day troubadour, similar to the traveling minstrels of the Middle Ages who told stories through song.

Like Mark Twain with a guitar instead of a cigar, or Will Rogers with a guitar instead of a lasso, Rogers regaled audiences with his tall tales, witticisms and homespun humor.

At festivals and music halls around the country, he told stories about colorful Southern characters like Still Bill and Agamemnon Jones, who lived in imaginary Southern towns. As Rogers strummed his guitar, he wove his characters into his songs.

A middle school in St. Augustine is named for Rogers. In 1998, Rogers was posthumously inducted into the Florida Artists Hall of Fame. His albums are available from the Gamble Rogers Memorial Foundation, in Gainesville, which maintains an online memorial to the one-of-a-kind artist (http://www.gamblerogers.com).

3
Central East Florida

Lue Gim Gong Memorial and Mural

Address: (Memorial) Henry A. DeLand House Museum, 137
W. Michigan Avenue, DeLand. (386) 740–6813. (Mural) 237 N.
Woodland Boulevard, DeLand. Volusia County.

Take the Yellow Brick Road and you'll find the Wizard of
Oz. Take the road to DeLand in western Volusia County
and you'll find reminders of the Citrus Wizard.

Horticulturalist Lue Gim Gong (1860–1925) earned that
nickname because of his citrus experiments and his development of the "Lue Gim Gong" orange around 1911. Gong's
fruit had an advantage of maturing before the onset of cold
weather.

Coincidentally, another DeLand resident, attorney Arthur
Hamlin, had developed the Hamlin orange around 1879,
notes Heller Bros. Packing Corp.

Lue's medium-size, seedless, frost-resistant Lue Gim
Gong orange, similar to a Valencia orange, earned him
the Wilder Silver Medal from the American Pomological
Society in 1911. It was a prestigious award never before given
to an American citizen for creating a new type of orange.
(Burnett 1986, Vol. 2, 18).

In addition to the nickname Citrus Wizard, Lue also was
referred to as "the Luther Burbank of Florida" because of his
work in plant breeding.

Lue Gim Gong was born in 1860 in Canton, China, to
parents who were farmers. When he was twelve years old,
he migrated to San Francisco. At age sixteen, he went to

Lue Gim Gong Memorial.

Massachusetts and took a job at C. T. Sampson, a shoe factory in North Adams, Massachusetts.

There, the course of his life was set when he enrolled in
Sunday school classes taught by Fannie Burlingame. Dis-
covering his skills with plants, she hired him to tend her
greenhouse.

Burlingame owned property in DeLand, so when she
moved there in 1886, she took Lue with her to care for her
citrus groves. He converted to Christianity and, in 1887, he
became an American citizen.

In 1903, "Mother Fannie," as Lue called her, died. For Lue's
years of service and friendship, Burlingame willed Lue her
property in DeLand, plus ten thousand dollars.

Lue continued experimenting with crosspollination and
tended to the orange and grapefruit trees and the plants

and flowers that he grew. In addition to the Lue Gim Gong orange, he produced a sweet-smelling grapefruit.

Bill Dreggors, a local historian with a wealth of knowledge about DeLand and executive director of the West Volusia Historical Society, says Lue wanted to marry a young Swedish girl, but her father forbade the marriage.

This was not so much because he didn't want his daughter to marry a Chinese man but rather because he wanted a Swedish grandson. The relationship was doomed.

In his old age, Lue was a frail white-haired man with three companions: his rooster, March, and his two horses, Baby and Fannie. March liked to ride around on Lue's shoulder.

"Lue didn't ride his two horses," says Dreggors. "He would walk and lead them into town. The sheriff told Lue that he had to ride the horses and not walk them, so Lue simply stopped coming into town.

"Instead, he hitched one of his horses to a wagon. One day, the horse stepped into a yellow-jacket nest. The horse

Lue Gim Gong Mural.

sought escape by heading into a lake while hitched to the wagon. Lue was thrown from the wagon and broke his hip. Thereafter, he couldn't walk without the aid of a crutch," notes Dreggors.

A devout Christian, Lue became a preacher. Using an orange crate as a pulpit, he led Sunday prayer services in a gazebo in his backyard. March was always there, perched on an orange crate.

"When Lue turned to March and announced, 'It's time to pray now,' the rooster stuck his head under his wing as though praying," says Dreggors.

Lue died in 1925 and was buried in Oakdale Cemetery, in DeLand. Elsewhere in the town, on N. Woodland Boulevard, there is a mural that is part of the DeLand Mural Walk. The mural shows the horticulturist standing in front of a citrus tree while holding his pet rooster. It was painted by local artist Courtney Canova.

The Lue Gim Gong Memorial Garden at the historic Henry DeLand House Museum features a replica of the wooden gazebo where Lue held prayer services. Inside the gazebo a bronze memorial bust of Lue rests on a stone pedestal.

A bronze plaque on the pedestal shows Lue striking the same pose as in the mural, accompanied by the images of a rising sun and a citrus tree. Also etched into the plaque are the words: "Lue Gim Gong. The Citrus Wizard. 1860–1925."

Carved into a wooden beam over the memorial is the proverb that guided Lue Gim Gong's life:

No one should live in this world for himself alone, but to do good for those who come after him.

Jackie Robinson Memorial

Address: Jackie Robinson Memorial Ball Park, 105 E. Orange Avenue, Daytona Beach. (386) 257–3172. Volusia County.

In 1945, Branch Rickey, general manager of the Brooklyn Dodgers, did something unthinkable for his time.

He signed young Jackie Robinson to a contract with the Dodgers baseball team. Until then, no African Americans had played with a major league baseball team. They played in the so-called Negro Leagues.

For Robinson, the baseball diamond was a field of dreams. However, he also knew that the sight of his dark skin in a sea of white faces would make that dream a field of prejudice, not only in the eyes of many Dodgers fans but in the eyes of his teammates as well.

According to sportswriter Maury Allen, teammates Carl Furillo and Dixie Walker resented Robinson in the beginning, but Robinson found support from teammates Duke Snider and Pee Wee Reese (Allen 1999).

Jack Roosevelt Robinson was a natural athlete. He was born in Georgia in 1919 and raised in Pasadena, California.

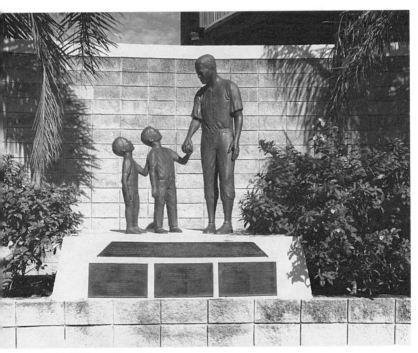

Jackie Robinson Memorial.

At the University of California in Los Angeles, he excelled in baseball, basketball, football and track.

On March 17, 1946, Robinson played for the Montreal Royals, the Dodgers' farm team, against the Dodgers at City Island Ballpark in Daytona Beach.

Florida's segregation laws prohibited Robinson from playing in any Florida city, but Daytona Beach was the home of the Brooklyn Dodgers' spring training camp, so the city permitted him to play.

This historic event was a boost for civil rights and a momentous occasion for professional sports because it was baseball's first racially integrated spring training game. It broke the color barrier and opened the door for future black baseball players.

Robinson again broke the barrier in 1947 by playing for the Brooklyn Dodgers at the team's own Ebbets Field.

Robinson won the National League batting title in 1946, a feat he repeated in 1947 while playing second base. In 1949, he was named the National League's Most Valuable Player. In 1962, he was inducted into the National Baseball Hall of Fame.

The polite, reserved history-making player with the number "42" on his uniform was adept at stealing bases, running and hitting. He led the Dodgers to six World Series and a World Series championship.

Robinson endured hate mail, hostility from other baseball players, threats on his life and racial obscenities from baseball fans but, with grace under pressure, he brought baseball into a new era, and his image grew more dignified and admirable.

"I'm not concerned with your liking or disliking me," he was quoted as saying. "All I ask is that you respect me as a human being."

In 1956, Robinson was traded to the San Francisco Giants but he quit baseball, apparently convinced that he had done enough for the game and it had done enough for him. He owned a men's clothing store, served as vice president of Chock full o'Nuts and championed causes focusing on racial equality.

Robinson died in 1972.

City Island Ball Park in Daytona Beach was renamed Jackie Robinson Ball Park in his honor. The ballpark features historical markers describing its history, especially in relation to Jackie Robinson.

In 1990, Robinson's widow Rachel dedicated a memorial statue of her husband as a reminder of his legacy to baseball. Located at the park's entrance, the bronze statue depicts Robinson with two young fans.

Baseball player Duke Snider once said of Jackie Robinson, "He was the greatest competitor I have ever seen." Many sports fans and historians would agree with his assessment.

Mary McLeod Bethune Memorial

Address: Mary McLeod Bethune Performing Arts Center, 640 Dr. Mary McLeod Bethune Boulevard, Daytona Beach. (386) 481-2774. Volusia County.

Mary McLeod Bethune was a big woman, not only in physical appearance, but in spirit and accomplishment.

During the twentieth century, she was one of Florida's and America's most important and influential black women. Given her humble origins, her achievements were remarkable.

Mary McLeod Bethune was born in Mayesville, South Carolina, in 1875 to Patsy and Samuel McLeod, former slaves who had become sharecroppers. Mary had sixteen siblings. She could not read as a child but she knew that books would lift her out of the fields and into a world of knowledge.

When a Presbyterian mission teacher came to the McLeods' home county, Mary walked for miles each day just to attend his classes. There, she learned to read.

Bright and curious, she qualified for a scholarship to a seminary. In 1895, she graduated from Moody Bible Institute, in Chicago.

Mary married Albert Bethune, a fellow teacher, and together they had one son, but the marriage didn't last. She moved to Florida in 1897 and took a teaching job in Palatka before settling in Daytona.

There she decided to open her own school to educate black students. This was a daunting goal for a woman who had no money. Bethune, however, had a steely will and a deep faith in God. She relied on both.

She settled on a dump site on the west side of the railroad tracks and convinced the owner of the land to sell it to her for two hundred dollars, payable in five-dollar monthly installments, according to the Halifax Historical Museum.

In 1899, Bethune established the Daytona Normal and Industrial School for Girls. With only $1.50 for supplies, she begged, borrowed and cajoled, sought donations and salvaged necessary items. If a packing crate had to serve as her desk, so be it.

Mary McLeod Bethune Memorial

When the school opened, Bethune had a handful of students to whom she charged fifty cents weekly tuition. In 1904, her school merged with the Cookman Institute for Boys, giving birth to Bethune Cookman College.

She transformed it into a three-million-dollar institution that she said she built "brick upon brick," notes the Halifax Historical Museum in its Mary McLeod Bethune exhibit. In the 1940s, author and anthropologist Zora Neale Hurston lectured at Bethune Cookman College. The board of trustees included such notables as James Gamble, son of the founder of Proctor and Gamble, and playwright Harrison Garfield Rhodes, both of whom resided in Volusia County.

The college's Rhodes Hall (now the School for Social Sciences) was named for Rhodes. When his wife Margaret died in 1959, she bequeathed more than half a million dollars to the school (Halifax, 3).

Bethune served as president of Bethune Cookman College from 1931 to 1942. She wrote articles and served on committees championing civil rights. She received honorary degrees from fourteen colleges and universities.

Bethune also served as President Roosevelt's advisor on minority affairs and became the highest-ranking appointee to his black cabinet, then known as the Office of Negro Affairs.

Bethune's connection to President Roosevelt led to her long-term friendship with First Lady Eleanor Roosevelt. Visitors who tour Bethune's home on the campus of Bethune Cookman College can see the bed in which Eleanor Roosevelt slept when she was Bethune's houseguest.

Bethune's correspondence, awards, honors and personal possessions are on display in the house, which is listed on the National Register of Historic Places. The grounds also contain her grave.

Located on South Beach Street in Daytona Beach, the Halifax Historical Museum features an exhibit case devoted to Bethune's life. One artifact attests to her popularity: a portrait doll with the likeness of her face.

When Bethune died in 1955, she was nearly eighty. Her last will and testament describes the ideals she strove to live up to and the legacy she hoped to leave to the world:

> I leave you love; love builds. . . . I leave you a thirst for education; knowledge is the prime need. . . . I leave you a desire to live harmoniously with your fellow man. We must learn to deal with people positively. I leave you responsibility to our young people. Our children must not lose their zeal for building a better world.

The Mary McLeod Bethune Performing Arts Center in Daytona Beach is a $23–million, 2,500–seat facility that opened in 2003. Outside, a twelve-foot-high bronze memorial statue of Bethune stands on a granite base. The $500,000 statue was sculpted by John Lajba of Omaha, Nebraska, notes the center.

The statue features this inscription:

> Thoughts from Dr. Mary McLeod Bethune upon seeing a rose garden in Bern, Switzerland, with Eleanor Roosevelt:
> ". . . This shall always be before me as a great interracial garden where men and women from all tongues, all nations, all creeds, all classes blend together helping to send out sunshine and love and peace and brotherhood that makes a better world in which to live."

AHEPA New Smyrna (Odyssey) Memorial

Address: Riverside Park, Canal Street and Riverside Drive, New Smyrna Beach. (386) 478–0052. Volusia County.

In 1768, five years after the British took control of the territory of Florida, Scottish physician Andrew Turnbull established a plantation colony in the southern part of what is
now Volusia County.

In honor of his wife's birthplace of Smyrna (now Izmir)
in Turkey, Turnbull named his colony New Smyrna. The
colony was located on twenty thousand acres granted to
Turnbull by the governor of British East Florida.

To work the plantation colony, Turnbull traveled to the
Aegean and recruited 200 tribesmen from Greece, 110
adventurous souls from Corsica, and hundreds more from
Minorca who were tired of famine in their homeland and
eager for a better life (Norwood's).

The new colonists agreed to farm the land as indentured
servants for seven years. At the end of their servitude, they
would receive fifty acres of land each. In 1768, more than a
thousand hopeful Greek, Sicilian and Minorcan recruits set
sail on a three-month journey to Florida.

During the difficult passage, 148 of the colonists died,
and when the rest of them arrived in New Smyrna Colony,
they encountered harsh living conditions because Turnbull
had not brought enough provisions (Foundation for New
Smyrna Museum of History).

Supplies were adequate for five hundred colonists, but
Turnbull had seduced more than twelve hundred people
into joining the colony. According to Constantine Rizo-
poulos, president of the American Hellenic Educational
Progressive Association (AHEPA) New Smyrna Memorial,
Inc., more than half the colonists had died from disease,
starvation or overwork by 1771. Many had ingested toxic
fumes from processing indigo.

Turnbull's financial problems running his New Smyrna
plantation had caused him to neglect the colonists' basic
needs. Their only hope was to escape.

In the spring of 1777, nearly one hundred outraged colonists trekked north to St. Augustine. They soon were fol-

AHEPA New Smyrna (Odyssey) Memorial.

lowed by hundreds more. They hoped that the governor of British East Florida, Patrick Tonyn, would free them from a cruelty that had gone on for too long.

Governor Tonyn released the colonists from their indenture and issued an arrest warrant for Turnbull. Abandoned by its colonists, the New Smyrna colony fell apart. It had lasted only nine years. Turnbull escaped to South Carolina, where he died in 1792 (Leonard, "Florida of the British").

Today on St. George Street in St. Augustine, visitors to the Saint Photios Greek Orthodox National Shrine can examine exhibits, documents, photographs and artifacts relating to the survivors of the New Smyrna settlement.

It seems that Turnbull's greed, indifference and poor money management were his (and the colonists') undoing. Despite his failures, he deserves credit for establishing one of the largest, earliest and most ambitious colonial plantation settlements in the New World.

For this reason, the Volusia County Historical Commission decided to honor him in the late 1960s with a permanent memorial. Located in front of New Smyrna Beach

City Hall, on Sams Avenue, the stone monument bears a bronze plaque with a profile of Andrew Turnbull and these words: "Dr. Andrew Turnbull, December 2, 1720 to March 13, 1792. Founder of the largest colony under British rule ever to come to the New World. The New Smyrna Colony of Florida, 1768 to 1778. Placed by the Volusia County Historical Commission, 1969."

Across from the Turnbull monument stands a stone memorial to the New Smyrna colonists. It was erected in 1968 by AHEPA. It is inscribed:

> Dedicated on the 200th anniversary in honor of those intrepid Hellenese who came to the New World in 1768 as settlers of the historic New Smyrna colony of Florida.
>
> By Americans proud of their Hellenic heritage, we cherish their participation in the great ideals of democracy and freedom as embodied in our American way of life, so that generations yet unborn may fulfill the hopes engendered by these priceless legacies.

More recently, AHEPA erected another, more striking memorial to the colonists. In Riverside Park, the AHEPA New Smyrna Memorial, also known as the Odyssey Memorial, is a white, Byzantine-style memorial to the Minorcans who were part of Turnbull's colony.

Above the memorial's arched entry, a design of multicolored stained glass represents organizations that contributed to the memorial. Carved into the marble walls are descriptions of the Minorcans' perilous New Smyrna odyssey, including this synopsis co-written by local residents T. C. Wilder, Joanne Sikes and Gary Luther:

> Food was rationed as the colonists were barely a month away from starvation. . . . Mosquitoes were merciless, death was a daily occurrence; 450 died in the first year.
>
> A rebellion involving Greek and Italian colonists erupted August 19, 1768. . . . Three of the leaders were found guilty. Two were hanged by the third, who was pardoned, serving as executioner. . . .
>
> In April 1777, 90 colonists . . . walked to St. Augustine and gave Governor Tonyn depositions of cruelty, ill treat-

ment and murder by the overseers. They were freed from their indentures. . . .

Within a month, 600 more deserted en masse to St. Augustine . . . they became merchants, fishermen and farmers. . . .

Today many St. Augustine residents can trace their ancestry to Minorcans who survived Andrew Turnbull's ambitious experiment.

Space Mirror (Astronauts Memorial)

Address: Kennedy Space Center Visitor Complex, S.R. 405, Titusville. (321) 449–4444. Brevard County.

The black granite surface looms more than forty-two feet high and fifty feet wide over a plaza at the Kennedy Space Center. This is the Space Mirror or "Astronauts Memorial," comprised of ninety granite, mirror-finished panels, each of which weighs five hundred pounds and is two inches thick (Astronauts Memorial Foundation).

The Space Mirror was dedicated in May 1991 in memory of United States astronauts who sacrificed their lives for the sake of space exploration. Engraved through the granite and filled with clear acrylic, the astronauts' names seem to float among the reflected clouds of the sky.

This national memorial is a project of the Astronauts Memorial Foundation (AMF), a living memorial to the astronauts. The AMF came into existence after the *Challenger* space shuttle explosion in 1986.

The AMF built and operates a 47,000–square-foot Center for Space Education and brings technology into local classrooms to pique students' interest and imaginations.

The foundation also established the Alan Shepard Technology in Education Award, named for the first astronaut to fly into space. It is awarded annually to a U.S. teacher or school administrator who has made the greatest contribution to the nation's educational technology.

Funding for the Space Mirror came from the proceeds of special *Challenger* commemorative license plates purchased by Florida residents after the *Challenger* disaster.

On January 28, 1986, seven astronauts died when their space shuttle, *Challenger*, exploded seventy-three seconds after liftoff from Kennedy Space Center. Investigators later determined that cold weather had cracked an O-ring on one of the *Challenger*'s solid rocket boosters, as described twenty years later in an article by Michael Browning (*Palm Beach Post*, January 28, 2006).

The names of every astronaut killed aboard the *Challenger* may not come readily to mind, but decades later and into a new century, Americans do remember one victim's

Space Mirror (Astronauts Memorial). Photo courtesy of Kennedy Space Center.

name: Sharon Christa McAuliffe, a high school teacher from Concord, New Hampshire. She was the nation's first teacher in space.

The City of Boynton Beach, Florida, paid tribute to McAuliffe by naming a middle school for her. Similarly, at Morikami Museum and Japanese Gardens, in Delray Beach, another *Challenger* astronaut is remembered in a placid spot shaded by simple plantings.

There a lantern-shaped traditional Japanese stone memorial pays tribute to Hawaiian-born Ellison Onizuka, a thirty-seven-year-old mission specialist who perished with the rest of the *Challenger* crew.

The names of *Challenger*'s astronauts are engraved on the Space Mirror memorial, as are those of the seven astronauts killed when the space shuttle *Columbia* exploded over Texas on February 1, 2003.

From Virgil "Gus" Grissom, who died in 1967 on *Apollo I,* to *Challenger*'s mission specialist Judith Resnik, the first Jewish astronaut in space, to Commander Rick Husband, who died aboard *Columbia*, twenty-four astronauts are memorialized on the Space Mirror.

Near the Space Mirror, a 6' × 6' granite memorial wall features biographies and photos of the twenty-four astronauts.

The wall and the Space Mirror memorial herald the courage and the spirit of the adventurous men and women who gave their lives in pursuit of the conquest of space.

American Police Hall of Fame Memorials

Address: 6350 Horizon Drive, Titusville. (321) 264–0911. Brevard County.

Before you enter the American Police Hall of Fame and Museum, in Titusville, notice the black granite slab by the front entrance. It's your first clue that the American Police Hall of Fame and Museum is about courage, bravery and dedication.

The granite slab is the museum's Canine (K-9) Memorial. The figure of a German shepherd is etched into the granite, along with these grateful words:

> Born to love, trained to serve, loyal to the end. Best friend to our nation's finest. We served our master who served mankind.
>
> Faithful to the end. An officer's extra senses to guide and protect. Our eyes in the dark. A nose for danger. A partner faithful beyond words.

At the bottom of the memorial appear these words:

> Dedicated to all canines who have died in the line of duty or who have served faithfully and have been retired from law enforcement duties.

When the sun hits the granite memorial, a reflection of the American Police Hall of Fame building appears in the background.

This effect makes the Canine Memorial that much more bittersweet because the reflected 50,000–square-foot facility is home to the nation's first memorial, museum and chapel honoring law officers who died in the line of duty.

Columns flank an archway leading to the law enforcement memorial inside the building. "Good men and women must die but death cannot kill their names" is written above the archway.

Inside, an American flag drapes a coffinlike marble rectangle bearing the words "dedicated to the unknown peace officer."

A marble memorial wall known as the Wall of Fame bears testimony to the sacrifices made by fallen law enforcement officers. Engraved there are the names of more than six thousand police officers from federal, state, county and local police departments who have died in the line of duty since 1960.

Adding to the poignancy are simple gestures of remembrance propped against the wall: a little teddy bear, a slim vase of flowers, a loving note from a child.

Visitors to the facility will learn that if all of the names on the four-hundred-ton marble wall were linked, they would stretch for more than one mile. That mile would continue to multiply as long as statistics remain the same: An American police officer is killed in the line of duty every fifty-seven hours.

Outside the Wall of Fame, there is a memorial bust of Miami Beach Police Department Detective Scott Rakow, who was killed during an undercover drug sting in June 1988.

On June 29, Rakow was in pursuit of a fleeing drug dealer when the dealer turned around and shot Rakow above his eye. Rakow, who was twenty-nine and had a six-month-old daughter, died the following day.

Rakow's death was instrumental in the passage in 1989 of the Law Enforcement Protection Act, informally known as the Scott Rakow Bill. This Florida law requires a minimum

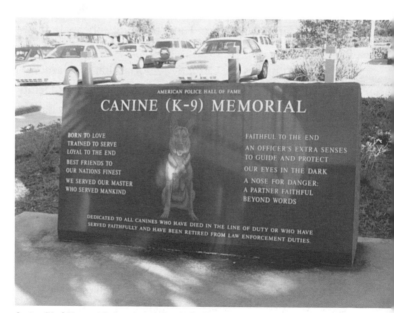

Canine (K-9) Memorial, American Police Hall of Fame and Museum.

Scott Rakow Memorial, American Police Hall of Fame and Museum.

mandatory sentence for anyone who commits a violent crime against members of law enforcement and against state attorneys.

The plaque on the bronze bust states: "In loving memory from your wife and daughter, mother and father, sister and brothers. A hero in life. Det. Scot Rakow. July 29, 1959–June 30, 1988."

The American Police Hall of Fame and Museum also is home to a 9/11 Memorial that honors the law enforcement officers who died on September 11, 2001. The memorial incorporates pieces of the World Trade Center buildings.

While the site's various memorials are touching and sad, its exhibits are fascinating. Given the popularity of TV shows like *CSI, Criminal Minds* and *NCIS*, visitors will be intrigued by how the museum examines the nature of crime.

There are a crime lab and a crime scene where you can test your detective skills. An exhibit about the Wild West includes Bat Masterson's pistol, a look at Judge Roy Bean and information about Western outlaws. Another exhibit focuses on the assassination of President John F. Kennedy.

Other intriguing exhibits include a kids' discovery and dress-up area, weaponry displays and police pursuit vehicles, including actor Harrison Ford's car from *Blade Runner*, to imprisonment and death devices.

Guess what Dr. Joseph Guillotine invented in 1792!

Paul Kroegel Memorial

Address: Riverview Park, Intersection of S.R. 512 and U.S. 1 at the foot of Indian River Lagoon, overlooking Pelican Island NWR, Sebastian. Indian River County. 772–562–3909

Were it not for Teddy Roosevelt, there may never have been national wildlife refuges in the United States.

Perhaps as important, if it were not for Paul Kroegel, Roosevelt may never have realized the need for such refuges nor established Pelican Island National Wildlife Refuge in Sebastian, Florida.

German immigrant Paul Kroegel was a teenager in 1881 when he came to live in Sebastian. His father built a house on top of a towering shell midden overlooking the Indian River.

The height of the midden gave Kroegel a good view of Pelican Island, a five-acre mangrove island that was a nesting and roosting ground for brown pelicans and other birds. Kroegel liked watching the birds. His interest in Pelican Island continued throughout his life.

Kroegel's fascination with pelicans was not only ornithological, it was humanitarian as well, explains the Pelican Island National Wildlife Refuge. Until the mid-1800s, thousands of birds had loafed undisturbed on Pelican Island. Then, the slaughters occurred.

Hunters seeking plumes for the fashion industry were boating to Pelican Island and killing dozens of roseate spoonbills. From his house, Kroegel looked toward the island and saw the killings.

Kroegel knew there was no one to protect the birds and no law to safeguard them, so he would take his boat—and gun—to Pelican Island to keep watch, according to the Pelican Island NWR web page.

In 1901, Kroegel became a warden for the Florida Audubon Society. He also met ornithologist Frank Chapman, who was curator at New York City's American Museum of Natural History. Kroegel told Chapman about the plight of the birds on Pelican Island and their need for protection.

Chapman was personally acquainted with Teddy Roose-

Paul Kroegel Memorial.

velt and knew that the president was a conservationist. The New York curator asked Roosevelt to protect Pelican Island.

On March 14, 1903, Roosevelt signed an executive order making Pelican Island the country's first National Wildlife Refuge (NWR). The birds of Pelican Island were now under federal protection. President Roosevelt established fifty-four NWRs during his eight years in the White House.

On April 1, 1903, at age thirty-nine, Kroegel became warden of Pelican Island, making him the nation's first wildlife warden.

Wearing his overalls and hat and carrying his gun, Kroegel became a familiar presence to the birds on Pelican Island. They learned to trust him and let him pat them.

In 1923, a hurricane diminished the island's bird population, and by 1926, Kroegel had relinquished his position as Pelican Island's wildlife warden.

Pelican Island has had a precarious past, despite its having been declared a national wildlife sanctuary. In 1918, for example, hundreds of baby pelicans were clubbed to death after commercial fishermen complained that pelicans were eating too many local fish. It turned out that the birds were no threat to the fishermen's livelihoods. The Florida Audubon Society conducted tests that indicated that most of the fish the birds were eating were commercially inconsequential.

Also, years of sea and wind forces eroded Pelican Island, but a restoration project helped retard the shoreline deterioration.

Pelican Island is located in the Indian River Lagoon, which has a reputation as the most biologically diverse estuary in the country. Pelican Island is now home to thirty species of birds, as well as turtles, manatees and other wildlife.

Covering more than five thousand acres and dotted with wetlands, mangroves, hammocks, marshes and wildlife, Pelican Island National Wildlife Refuge is a stunning paean to nature.

In 2003, in tribute to Pelican Island's centennial, the U.S. Postal Service issued a commemorative first-class stamp in Sebastian that bore the profile of a pelican.

Today visitors to Sebastian can stop by a memorial to Paul Kroegel located in Riverview Park. The life-size bronze statue depicts the nation's first wildlife warden looking over Indian River Lagoon, two brown pelicans gathered at his feet. The memorial inscription reads:

> One person can make a difference. Paul Kroegel 1864–1928. Audubon warden 1902. First Refuge warden 1903–1926. Pelican Island National Wildlife Refuge established March 14, 1903.

Governor Dan McCarty Monument

Address: Near the corner of U.S. 1 and Avenue A, outside Fort Pierce City Hall, Fort Pierce. St. Lucie County.

When thirty-two-year-old Dan McCarty hit the beach at Normandy on D-Day, June 6, 1944, he had no idea that nine years later he would serve one of the shortest terms in office as governor of Florida.

During World War II, McCarty served in the U.S. Seventh Army, attaining the rank of colonel. He earned the Purple Heart, the Legion of Merit, the Bronze Star and the French Croix de Guerre, notes the St. Lucie Historical Society. To many Floridians, he was a political hero and a war hero.

Dan McCarty served as governor of Florida for about nine months. He took office in January 1953 and had a heart attack in February.

Governor Dan McCarty Monument.

From February until his death from pneumonia the following September, McCarty continued to carry out his gubernatorial duties, primarily from a bed in the governor's mansion, reported a *Time* magazine obituary.

Daniel Thomas McCarty was born and raised in Fort Pierce, Florida. His boyhood home still stands on Indian River Drive. As a high school student he scored high both academically and athletically, as captain of the football team, as vice-president of his class and as editor-in-chief of the school yearbook.

McCarty's 1930 high school yearbook refers to him as "the captain of our school ship of state—and how able a captain," notes the St. Lucie Historical Society's home page. McCarty graduated from the University of Florida College of Agricultural and Life Sciences and became a citrus grower and cattleman. The administrative office of the University of Florida Institute of Food and Agricultural Sciences became known as McCarty Hall.

A Democrat, McCarty entered the world of politics as a representative of St. Lucie County in the Florida House of Representatives in 1937 and then in 1939 and 1941. In the latter year, at the young age of twenty-nine, he became speaker of the house. He temporarily abandoned politics to serve in the U.S. Army but resumed his career after distinguishing himself in the war.

Although his term as governor was brief, McCarty managed to accomplish numerous goals. He increased Florida's share from dog track betting in the state; he signed into law the Florida State Turnpike Act, initiating construction of the Florida Turnpike; he approved increases in teacher's salaries; and he set up aid programs for the disabled.

After McCarty died, his body was placed in the rotunda of the state capitol so his peers and the public could pay their respects. He is buried in Palms Cemetery, near Ankona in St. Lucie County.

Charley Johns, president of the Florida Senate, became acting governor of Florida from September 28, 1953, to January 4, 1955, when Thomas Leroy Collins was elected the state's thirty-third governor.

A stretch of U.S. 1 from Fort Pierce to Vero Beach was named McCarty Memorial Highway. A year after McCarty's death, a new high school opened in St. Lucie County. It was named Daniel T. McCarty High School.

A monument stands in front of the old city hall in Mc-Carty's hometown. Beneath his bronze profile are inscribed these words:

Dedicated to one of Florida's favorite sons. Statesman. Valiant soldier. Governor of Florida. Born January 18, 1912, Fort Pierce, Florida. Died September 28, 1953, while governor. Dedicated February 23, 1956, by Leroy Collins, Governor.

The Sabal palm is Florida's state tree. We can thank Dan McCarty for that. In Cascades Park on Bloxham Street, in Tallahassee, there is a small, ground-level stone memorial befittingly placed under a Sabal palm tree. It reads:

In memory of Gov. Dan McCarty, signer of Bill designating Sabal palmetto as Florida State tree June 11, 1953. Florida Federation of Garden Clubs, February 1954.

Four months after signing the bill, McCarty died. He was forty-one years old.

CeeCee Ross Lyles (United Flight 93) Memorial

Address: Liberty Garden Memorial Park, at the north end of Fort Pierce Community Center. 600 N. Indian River Drive, Fort Pierce. (Community Center: 772-462-1792.) St. Lucie County.

September 11, 2001. The infamous date is branded in the American consciousness. That morning, United Airlines Flight 93 departed Newark and headed for San Francisco. Somewhere near Cleveland, the Boeing 757 turned around.

Much has been written and filmed about what happened on United Flight 93, and what the world knows is based largely on cell phone calls that passengers and crew frantically made to their loved ones on the ground.

We know that terrorists on a suicide mission took control of the plane and we surmise that the terrorists who gained control of the cockpit planned to crash the plane into one of the heartbeats of our country—perhaps the White House, perhaps the U.S. Capitol.

We know that there were acts of great courage aboard Flight 93. Some passengers secretly planned to overtake the terrorists. One of those passengers was Todd Beamer, who is credited with giving the signal, "Let's roll!"

We also know from newspaper accounts that among the frightened passengers and crew, flight attendant CeeCee Lyles called her husband Lorne at home, but he was asleep. She left a message on the answering machine for him. She said she hoped she would see his face again.

CeeCee Lyles was able to call Lorne a second time. He answered the phone. She told him her plane had been hijacked. At first, Lorne thought she was joking, but her desperate words and the background noises he heard quickly convinced him otherwise.

The anxious flight attendant told her husband that she loved him and their children. Lorne Lyles was a police officer. His job was to protect people, but he knew there was nothing he could do at that moment to protect and save his wife. We can only imagine how anguished and helpless he must have felt.

CeeCee Ross Lyles (United Flight 93) Memorial.

CeeCee and Lorne Lyles were married in 2000. They each had two children from previous relationships. At the time of their marriage, each worked for the Fort Pierce Police Department, she as a detective, he as a police officer.

The couple moved to Fort Myers. Lorne took a job with the local police department. CeeCee became a flight attendant for United Airlines. It was an opportunity to do some traveling and to have a less stressful job. In the end, she would be a flight attendant for less than one year.

Aboard United Flight 93, passengers who rushed the skyjackers could not stop the plane from crashing but they succeeded in diverting it from its target. The aircraft went down in a field not far from Pittsburgh. There were no survivors. CeeCee Lyles was thirty-three years old when she died.

In the days and weeks that followed, the nation mourned. The world mourned. In all, four American airliners had been skyjacked on September 11, 2001. Two crashed into the World Trade Center in Manhattan. One crashed into the Pentagon. Another was United Flight 93.

In the aftermath of that unforgettably tragic day, Lorne Lyles was quoted in newspapers, on television, and on the Wall of Americans web site, and perhaps nothing he said is as poignant and heartbreaking as this: "Just hearing my wife saying she loved us through all that chaos on the plane is just embedded in my heart forever. That's my baby. She's my heart, she's my soul, she is my everything. That's my memory."

On a pine-tree-shaded stretch of grassland next to the Fort Pierce Community Center, a life-size bronze statue of CeeCee Lyles overlooks the Indian River Lagoon. Created by artist Chris Riccardo, the sculpture depicts Lyles wearing her flight attendant uniform, including a United logo pin. Her left hand is on her hip and she is smiling, as though posing for a picture. The back of the statue is inscribed, "To the memory of September 11, 2001."

To the right of the statue, a granite memorial plaque rests on a stone base. A likeness of a smiling CeeCee Lyles is etched into the shiny black granite, which, appropriately, reflects the clouds above. Lyles' job carried her into the skies.

These words are engraved in the granite:

In loving memory of CeeCee Ross Lyles. November 26, 1967–September 11, 2001. Our American Hero. Flight attendant on United Airlines 'Flight 93' and former Fort Pierce police officer. We will never forget you. Your family, friends and community.

Navy UDT-SEAL ("Naked Warrior") Memorial

Address: National Navy UDT-SEAL Museum, 3300 N. Highway (S.R.) A1A, North Hutchinson Island, Fort Pierce. (772) 595–5845. St. Lucie County.

He stands naked except for his swim trunks, face mask, knife and swim fins. This is the "Naked Warrior" or Navy SEAL. He is a life-size bronze sculpture standing on a base in a shallow pool of water in front of the National Navy UDT-SEAL Museum, in Fort Pierce.

The inscription on the base reads:

> In memory of our fallen comrades who sacrificed their lives in the service of their country while serving in the United States Navy with Naval Combat Demolition Units, Scouts and Raiders, Underwater Demolition Teams and Sea, Air, Land Teams.

During World War II, many U.S. Marines were killed because of obstacles that hindered their landing craft from reaching targeted beaches. This problem gave birth to a new concept: hydrographic reconnaissance and underwater demolition. The National Navy UDT-SEAL Museum tells the story of this eventful chapter in American military history.

Between 1943 and 1945, hundreds of servicemen trained in combat demolition at a naval base on Florida's South Hutchinson Island and on the beaches of North Hutchinson Island, where the National Navy UDT-SEAL Museum now stands.

These volunteers were nicknamed "Frogmen" because they were trained as combat swimmers to accomplish their mission. Teams of Frogmen, called Naval Combat Demolition Units (NCDUs), became Underwater Demolition Teams (UDTs) later in World War II.

On D-Day, June 6, 1944, these volunteers swam onto Utah and Omaha beaches in Normandy, France. In the Pacific, they were on Iwo Jima and Okinawa and countless other islands in the region, blowing up the enemy's underwater mines and clearing beach obstacles to make way for the amphibious landings of U.S. Marines.

Navy UDT-SEAL ("Naked Warrior") Memorial.

During the Korean War, UDTs conducted demolition raids against railroads, bridges and tunnels and swept mines from the harbors and rivers. In 1962, select UDT members were transformed into Sea, Air and Land (SEAL) teams. These men conducted guerrilla warfare and gathered intelligence in Vietnam.

The training base on North Hutchinson Island closed in 1946 after the end of World War II. Navy SEALs now train on the beaches of Coronado, California, and underwater in San Diego Bay. They undergo a rigorous, extensive and exhausting twenty-three-week-long training program divided into three separate phases.

The most grueling phase is the first—"Hell Week," a carryover from the early training classes given during World War II. Hell Week is a challenge to the mind and body. It helps determine which students are committed to becoming a Navy SEAL.

The National Navy UDT-SEAL Museum describes Navy SEALs as "the most elite commando force in the world." The Naked Warriors have continued to employ their underwater demolition skills around the globe. Hollywood has glorified their heroism.

The 1951 movie *The Frogmen*, starring Richard Widmark, Dana Andrews and Robert Walker, gave audiences a window into the dangers faced by UDTs paving the way for the Allied invasion of a Japanese-held island during World War II (Halliwell 1991).

Made nearly forty years later, the film *Navy SEALs* (1990), starring Charlie Sheen, depicts SEALs up against Middle Eastern terrorists while on a mission to destroy a weapons arsenal in Lebanon.

The National Navy UDT-SEAL Museum tells the story of U.S. Naval Special Warfare via photographs, storyboards, weapons, other artifacts and videos. Volunteers are on hand to answer questions. For visitors old enough to remember past decades and for those too young to have known, the museum is a testimony to heroism.

Beach obstacles used for training during World War II are on display on the museum grounds, along with a Vietnam-era Bell UH-1 "Huey" helicopter and several watercraft, including a Patrol Boat, River/Riverine, better known as a "PBR."

Memorial bricks purchased by current and former SEALs and various museum supporters form a border around the walkways. One brick is inscribed, "in memory of my swim buddy."

The museum hosts an annual Muster on Veterans Day weekend that attracts thousands of former SEALs, servicemen and civilians.

Among them is Navy SEAL Rudy Boesch, who trained on the beaches of Fort Pierce and who was one of the finalists in the first season of the TV reality show *Survivor*.

The activities include demonstrations by SEAL snipers, aerial flyovers, precision parachute jumps by the "Leapfrogs" (the Navy's and SEALs' elite parachute team), rappelling from helicopters and demolition demonstrations.

At the end of the weekend, a memorial service is held for all the UDT and SEAL team veterans who passed away during the year. The museum is a fitting setting for the service, explains its curator Ruth McSween:

"Many of these veterans trained on the beach in Fort Pierce . . . and have expressed their wishes to have their ashes scattered at sea during this ceremony. It's a solemn reminder of the personal sacrifices these individuals made during their time of service to their country," she adds.

On August 28, 2006, the *Palm Beach Post* reported that a man diving off Hutchinson Island found a rusted-over World War II-era bomb, most of it intact. He put it into his truck and drove to a fire station. Law enforcement officials then detonated the bomb.

This episode illustrates the potential dangers for divers and treasure hunters who know that navy Frogmen trained in this area and who come here in search of World War II artifacts.

Okeechobee Battlefield Monument

**Address: Okeechobee Battlefield Historic State Park, U.S. 441
South, about one and a half miles south of Taylor Creek. Park
is located on a 145–acre site off SE 38th Avenue, across from the
Treasure Island Fire Station, Okeechobee County. 561–744–9814**

During the Thanksgiving week of 1837, Colonel Zachary
Taylor and his men left Fort Brooke in Tampa on a mission
to find some four thousand Seminoles still living in Florida.

This was during the Second Seminole War, when the
federal Indian Removal Act required that all remaining
Seminole and Miccosukee tribes be removed from Florida
and relocated west of the Mississippi River.

Taylor knew that many Seminoles had a camp to the east.
He and his men were on the move for a month when they
finally reached the northern shore of Lake Okeechobee on
December 25, 1837. It was there that a band of four hundred
Seminole and Miccosukee warriors attacked Taylor's troops.

Spearheading the ambush were the noted Seminole
leaders Chief Alligator, medicine man Abiaka (a.k.a. Sam
Jones) and Chief Coacoochee, known as "Wild Cat" among
white soldiers. A few weeks prior to the battle, Wild Cat had
escaped from his prison cell at Fort Marion (Castillo de San
Marcos), in St. Augustine (Burnett 1986, Vol. 2, 114).

Coacoochee was of royal Seminole blood. His father
was Chief King Phillip. His mother was the sister of Chief
Micanopy.

The battle lasted for several hours, and when the Seminoles finally fled, Taylor's forces, numbering one thousand,
including many Missouri Volunteers, had suffered consider-
ably more casualties than had the Seminoles.

Twenty-six soldiers lay dead and 112 were wounded. On
the Seminole side, eleven had been killed, and fourteen lay
wounded.

Coacoochee continued to fight the Indian Removal Act
and later was quoted as saying, "I had rather be killed by a
white man in Florida than die in Arkansas" (Burnett, 1986,
Vol. 2, 114).

Four years after the Battle of Okeechobee, Coacoochee could no longer bear the starvation and constant uprooting of the Seminole women and children.

He surrendered to Colonel William Jenkins Worth (for whom Palm Beach's Worth Avenue and the towns of Lake Worth, Florida, and Fort Worth, Texas, are named). With a heavy heart, Coacoochee made the move to Arkansas.

Zachary Taylor, a pivotal player in the Battle of Okeechobee and in previous and ensuing battles, earned the nickname "Old Rough and Ready." Fort Zachary Taylor in Key West is named for him.

Born in Virginia in 1784, Taylor went on to become a hero of the Mexican War, in which he led and won several campaigns. His wartime exploits probably helped get him elected twelfth president of the United States in 1849.

That election involves an obscure morsel of historic trivia:

When President James Polk's term of office expired in 1849, his successor, Zachary Taylor, refused on religious grounds to take the presidential oath on a Sunday and delayed the ceremony to the following day.

On that Sunday, Senator David Atchison, for whom Atchison, Kansas, is named, served as president pro tempore of the U.S. Senate. Some historians say that Atchison became president of the United States for twenty-four hours. Others say that he never took the presidential oath (*Appleton's* 1887).

Nevertheless, America's smallest presidential library is located in Atchison, Kansas, all because Taylor refused to be sworn in until Monday.

Another piece of trivia is that in 1835, Taylor's daughter Sarah married Jefferson Davis, the future president of the Confederacy.

Zachary Taylor served only one year as president of the United States. He died of cholera in 1850.

At Okeechobee Battlefield Historic State Park, a boulder serves as a monument to the battle. The plaque on the boulder reads:

> In these woods on Christmas Day, 1837, was fought the
> Battle of Okeechobee in which a large band of Seminole
> Indians . . . was routed by a brigade led by Colonel Zachary

Taylor, consisting of the First, Fourth and Sixth Regiments of Infantry of the Regular Army, and the First Regiment of Missouri Volunteers totaling about 800 men.

Fighting was close, desperate and bloody. . . . This action was the turning point of . . . Indian resistance in Florida.

Officers who lost their lives were Colonel Richard Gentry of the Missouri Volunteers; Capt. Joseph Van Swearingen; . . . all of the Sixth Infantry Regular Army. . . . Dedicated through funds given by the descendants of Colonel Richard Gentry, and the Florida Society of the DAR.

Okeechobee Battlefield Historic State Park is a National Historic Landmark Site. It is listed on the National Register of Historic Places. The National Trust has recognized it as one of America's most endangered historical sites.

In April 2006, then-governor Jeb Bush and the Florida Cabinet approved the purchase of 145 acres in the Okeechobee Battlefield Florida Forever Project.

This is a ten-year three-billion-dollar project established by Governor Bush and the Florida Legislature to preserve

Okeechobee Battlefield Monument. Photo by Gary Ritter; courtesy of South Florida Water Management District.

Florida's important cultural and historic resources (State of Florida, Department of Environmental Protection, April 4, 2006).

Still in developmental stages, the park eventually will have a dedicated park ranger, an information and education center and kiosks throughout the 145 acres.

The Battle of Okeechobee was the bloodiest battle of the Second Seminole War. National Trust for Historic Preservation President Richard Moe was quoted as saying, "the blood of Native Americans and U.S. soldiers soaked its ground during that terrible fight.

"We owe it to those fallen men and their descendants to save it for future generations" (Okeeinfo 2004).

4

Southeast Florida

A.A. "Buck" Hendry, Jr., Memorial

Address: In front of Kiwanis Park, between SE Fifth Street and S. Colorado Avenue, Stuart. Martin County.

In downtown Stuart, a clock is ticking. It resembles many town clocks, but this one is dedicated to a Stuart businessman who was so admired and loved by the people of his city that they created a timepiece memorial to him.

The top of the fifteen-foot-tall black clock reads, "Dedicated to A. A. 'Buck' Hendry, Jr." At the base of the clock, a plaque with the outline of a ten-gallon hat is inscribed:

> In loving memory of A. A. 'Buck' Hendry, Jr., 1903–1990. A true pioneer who represented so much of what Stuart was in the past. We wish to recognize his many contributions to making this community what it is today.
> Al and Karen Hendry and Family.

Buck Hendry was born in Fort Pierce, St. Lucie County. He moved to Jensen Beach in 1930 and lived in Martin County until his death at age eighty-seven.

Buck's son A. A. (Al) Hendry III says his father's life was all about service to the community. Buck worked for Martin County at various times as a road superintendent, fire chief, purchasing agent and building inspector. Buck also headed the land department for the Central and South Florida Flood Control District and in that role he purchased one million acres of land for the district.

Al says his family roots in Florida go back to the 1800s. In the 1870s, the Hendry family moved to the Fort Pierce area

A. A. "Buck" Hendry, Jr., Memorial.

from Polk County. Al's grandfather, a boy at the time, grew up to become a cattleman.

Even as members of the Hendry family spread out across the state, there was always time for clan get-togethers. Al remembers that his father attended family reunions in Fort Myers, in Lee County. Because there were Hendry members established for generations in different parts of Florida, Al says it is likely that a branch of his family tree extends to the famed Florida cattleman Francis Hendry, for whom Hendry County was named.

Like Buck Hendry, Francis Hendry was equally adept at cattle roping and public service, and even though no clock ticks for him in downtown Stuart, his life story reveals much about Florida's history as well.

Francis Asbury Hendry was born in 1833. He fought in the Third Seminole War and the Civil War and provided the Confederate army with beef.

Francis Hendry reportedly owned fifty thousand head of cattle, which may explain why by 1876 he had developed a reputation as "Cattle King of South Florida," notes Spessard Stone in his Cracker Barrel genealogy site. (Included in the Web site's profiles of notable Southerners are biographies of eighteen Hendry family members.)

Francis Hendry served as a county commissioner in Hillsboro, Polk and Lee counties and was elected to Florida's Senate and House of Representatives. When a new county was formed from Monroe County in 1887, he proposed that it be named Lee County, in honor of Robert E. Lee. His motion was adopted (Stone 2001–2007)

Francis Hendry laid out the town of LaBelle in 1895. According to Stone, the name is a combination of "Laura" and "Belle," the names of Hendry's two daughters. LaBelle is now the seat of Hendry County, which was carved from Lee County.

1928 Hurricane (Belle Glade 1928) Monument

Address: 530 S. Main Street, Belle Glade. Palm Beach County.

The monument alongside the Belle Glade branch of the Palm Beach County Public Library is, in some respects, a study in panic. It honors the victims of a 1928 hurricane.

A wild scene is etched into the stone base: Surging waters smash into houses as distant palm trees tremble and bend. The base is inscribed "Belle Glade 1928."

The 7½–foot sculpture above the pedestal depicts events on the night of September 16, 1928, when a hurricane roared and ripped and caused Lake Okeechobee to overflow. The rushing waters flooded Belle Glade and surrounding areas known as the Glades.

The bronze sculpture commemorating the disaster was created by Ferenc Varga and his son Frank, and was dedicated in 1976. It depicts a family—a child, a father and a mother with a baby in her arms—as they flee the wrath of the hurricane.

The figures are in a running position. The parents' raised arms seem to be protectively shielding their faces from the fierce wind and rain. The sculpture is powerful, giving the observer an almost visceral connection to the figures.

In the 1920s, as it is today, Belle Glade was primarily a rural agricultural area where the fields were tended by migrant labor that worked the sugar cane and vegetable fields. The town's motto has always been "Her soil is her fortune." When the infamous 1928 storm stuck, however, the area's famous "black gold" became a muddy river of sorrow.

The Memorial Web Page of the National Weather Service's Weather Forecast Office in Miami recaptures the path and the aftermath of the 1928 Okeechobee Hurricane. In September 1928, the category 4 hurricane formed off the coast of Africa, whipped across the Caribbean and the Bahamas and eventually made landfall in Palm Beach County. Winds were estimated to have reached 150 miles per hour.

The southern end of Lake Okeechobee overflowed and flooded about seventy-five miles of farmland, including

1928 Hurricane ("Belle Glade 1928") Monument.

areas of Belle Glade, Canal Point, Pahokee and South Bay. Most of the people who drowned were migrant workers.

The hurricane then swept in a northwest direction across Lake Okeechobee and continued into Florida's south central and north central counties, as well as into Georgia, the Carolinas and Virginia.

The Johnstown (Pennsylvania) Flood of 1889 reportedly claimed about 2,200 victims. The Lake Okeechobee Hurricane of 1928 is estimated to have killed about 2,500 people, making it one of the nation's deadliest natural disasters.

Furthermore, in terms of property damage, injuries and loss of life, the 1928 hurricane's damage would equal about 16 billion in today's dollars.

After the hurricane, the Glades scene, racked with debris and dead bodies, was one of turmoil and destruction. It took weeks for rescue workers and cleanup crews to find many of the victim's bodies. Wooden caskets, some piled five caskets high, lined many of the streets.

Even today, Florida reporters covering natural disasters draw on comparisons to the Okeechobee tragedy. For example, in an article "Catastrophe Clouds Debate over Whether Dike Will Hold" (Palm Beach Post, May 14, 2006), reporter John Lantigua recounted stories of survivors who had frantically clung to life during the 1928 hurricane. These brave souls included one woman who, with one hand, held fast to her two children while her other hand desperately gripped an unstable tree branch throughout the night.

African American author and folklorist Zora Neale Hurston lived for a time in Belle Glade and she describes the horrific 1928 hurricane in her novel *Their Eyes Were Watching God*.

Elisha Newton "Cap" Dimick Memorial

Address: Located on the grassy median across from Society of the Four Arts, Royal Palm Way, Palm Beach. Palm Beach County.

Elisha Newton "Cap" Dimick was a Palm Beach pioneer and one of the town's most influential and admired residents. He was born in Michigan in 1849. In 1875, Dimick and his family came to Florida and settled in Jacksonville, where Dimick was involved in a broom-making business.

According to an article about Palm Beach history by writer Elizabeth Doup, Dimick heard about a freshwater lake in South Florida and was inspired to relocate there (*Palm Beach Times*, February 27, 1974).

He packed up the family's belongings, including a mule, and sailed by schooner from Jacksonville to West Palm Beach, which was then part of Dade County.

Doup's article quotes Claude Reese, Dimick's grandson, as saying that in those early days, if a homesteader occupied land for five years, the land was his.

To claim as much land as possible, Dimick would occupy one part of the land he wanted while his wife occupied another part of it. The Dimicks ended up owning six hundred acres for which he paid about $1200.

Dimick's wife Ella apparently settled into life as a pioneer wife. "Treasured Thanksgiving Traditions," an un-bylined article published in a Palm Beach newspaper in 1982, reveals that Ella squeezed scrub cactus to produce food coloring for the candied grapefruit and orange rinds she made for Thanksgivings (*Evening Times*, November 24, 1982).

Dimick built a fifteen-room hotel called Cocoanut Grove House. It was the only hotel in Palm Beach, and perhaps its most famous guest was Henry Flagler, who had come to Palm Beach to inspect the area as a possible location for a luxury hotel he planned to build.

Indeed, Flagler's future Breakers Hotel would turn Palm Beach into a ritzy winter vacation destination for the cream of society, but Dimick, whose name is unfamiliar to most people today, also left his footprint on Palm Beach.

Elisha Newton "Cap" Dimick Memorial.

Dimick was elected to the Florida Legislature in 1890. Six years later, he became a state senator. In 1893, he established Dade County State Bank. When Palm Beach County was formed from Dade County in 1909, the bank was renamed Pioneer Bank.

In 1911, Dimick was part of a committee that formed the Town of Palm Beach and that same year, he was elected Palm Beach's first mayor, a position he held until 1918. He died a year later at age seventy.

"Mayor" appears to be a dynastic title for the Dimick family, noted the city's paper (*Palm Beach Times*, December 2, 1970).

Thomas Tipton Reese, Sr., who married Dimick's daughter Belle at Royal Poinciana Chapel in December 1895, became mayor of Palm Beach, as did their son Claude D. Reese. Claude served as mayor for eighteen years.

Today a life-size bronze statue of Elisha Newton "Cap" Dimick greets people exiting the bridge from Flagler Drive in West Palm Beach onto Royal Palm Way in Palm Beach. The first mayor of Palm Beach stands in his coat and tie, welcoming visitors to one of America's most illustrious shopping streets. The plaque on the base of the statue is inscribed:

> In honor and memory of Elisha Newton Dimick. A pioneer who served his community well. Legislator, developer and friend. 1849–1919.

John Prince Memorial Park

Address: 2700 Sixth Avenue South, Lake Worth. (561) 966–6600. Palm Beach County.

In 1937, Floridian John Prince had a vision. He saw hundreds of acres of land surrounding Lake Osborne, a freshwater lake in Lake Worth, and he thought that the entire area could be turned into a county park for the public to enjoy.

Prince was a member of the Palm Beach County Board of Commissioners, so he told the other commissioners about his idea. They adopted a resolution that asked the State of Florida to relinquish its ownership of the lake and the land surrounding it and to deed all of it to Palm Beach County.

Prince traveled to Tallahassee, where he met with Governor Fred Cone to present the commission's request. As reported by Nancy Powell in the *Palm Beach Post-Times*, Governor Cone told Prince that the state was not in the habit of giving away land rather than selling it ("John Prince: The Man and the Park," March 21, 1971).

However, the apparently sympathetic governor advised Prince to come back with the deeds from the owners of the land west of Lake Osborne, because those owners had first option to buy the state land that Prince wanted.

The *Palm Beach Post-Times* also reported that Prince discovered that the Phipps family and the Model Land Development Company owned the land west of the lake. It would be up to Prince to convince them to give up the deeds.

Prince was passionate and persuasive and, months later, he returned to Tallahassee, this time with what surely was a sense of triumph.

In her story on John Prince and the development of the park, writer Nancy Powell also quotes Prince's statement to the state's Internal Improvement Board: "There you are, gentlemen—deeds to the land, gifts from the Model Land Company and the Phipps interests. Now the deed, if you please" (*Palm Beach Post Times*, March 21, 1971).

Lake Osborne, John Prince Memorial Park.

Those who knew Prince would probably say that, given his dedication to Palm Beach County, this triumph was not surprising. He had begun to demonstrate his commitment to improving his community as a young man fresh out of high school.

Within two years of graduating Peter Stuyvesant High School in New York City, where he was born in 1892, Prince had moved to what we now know as Lake Worth, Florida.

There, in 1912, he began his longtime connection with county improvements and developments and his involvement with local civic groups and fraternal organizations.

Prince worked for the county engineer's office and helped clear land for the development of a town called Lucerne, which was later renamed Lake Worth.

He became involved with numerous park and road construction projects. In 1916, he became an inspector for the county's road department during the construction of Dixie Highway. He served on the Palm Beach County Board of Commissioners for eighteen years.

In 1952, Prince suffered a stroke and died shortly after. He was the widower of Mary Rouse Prince. He was survived by their daughter Margaret.

Prince was buried on June 14, 1952, in Pinecrest Cemetery, in Lake Worth. All that day the county's courthouse was to be closed in tribute to him, noted the *Palm Beach Post* (June 12, 1952).

Exactly one month after Prince's death, the Board of County Commissioners of Palm Beach County adopted Resolution No. 0028142, stating:

> The late Honorable John Prince . . . was the first proponent of a public park system in Palm Beach County . . . and has given . . . effort throughout his career . . . to providing public parks for the enjoyment and recreation of the citizens of the County. . . . [T]he Board deems it fitting . . . that the memory of this distinguished public official be honored by naming the first County Park for him.

Encompassing more than 725 acres, including the 338–acre Lake Osborne, John Prince Memorial Park offers myriad sports and recreation venues for residents to enjoy. That's exactly what Prince had intended.

C. Spencer Pompey Memorial

Address: Inside Delray Beach City Hall, 100 NW First Avenue, Delray Beach. Palm Beach County.

C. Spencer Pompey, who lived in Delray Beach, had a far-reaching impact on the cause of civil rights. That impact helped strengthen the career of a young black lawyer who eventually became a justice of the United States Supreme Court.

In 1941, a coalition of Palm Beach County black school-teachers, spearheaded by fellow teacher C. Spencer Pompey, brought a class-action suit against the county for equal pay.

According to Pompey's widow Ruth, the county had rewarded white teachers with a twenty-five-dollar raise but had given nothing to black teachers.

C. Spencer Pompey Memorial. Photo courtesy of George Gadson.

Ruth Pompey says the group brought suit in federal court in Fort Pierce and used the Fourteenth amendment—the Equal Protection Clause—as their legal basis. "The NAACP sent a young lawyer to the group to try the case," Pompey says. "His name was Thurgood Marshall."

They won the suit. Marshall would go on to become a justice of the United States Supreme Court.

"Pompey and the other teachers not only went for equalization of teachers' salaries, but for equalization of opportunities in the classroom," she notes.

C. Spencer Pompey was revered by Delray Beach residents because of his principles, integrity and community involvement. Until his death in 2001, he worked to further race relations.

Former Delray Beach mayor Jeff Perlman thinks Pompey was a hero. "When I ran for office in 2000, he was one of the first people I visited," says Perlman. " I asked if he thought I had what it took to be effective.

"If he said no, I wouldn't have run. That's how much I valued his judgment. But he said yes, that I could and should run, and his blessing proved to be an inspiration in my campaign."

According to Ruth Pompey, C. Spencer Pompey was born in Live Oak in Suwannee County in 1915. He graduated from Johnson C. Smith University in North Carolina and the University of Minnesota. He took his first teaching job in Live Oak.

From there, he became principal of two black schools, a three-teacher school in Lake Park and a junior high school in Boynton Beach.

At the close of World War II, Pompey went to another black school, Carver High, as head of the social studies department. "He asserted his greatest influence on the community through his civics and government classes," Ruth Pompey says.

Pompey instituted a sports program at Carver and a summer recreational program on a tract of local land that the City of Delray Beach later named C. Spencer Pompey Park in his honor. Pompey later became principal of Seacrest High School in Boynton Beach.

According to Ruth Pompey, in the 1940s, the local black schools were given old books while students in white schools received new books. This inequitable practice prompted Pompey to write an updated syllabus for his students.

"Pompey was highly principled and modest," she says. "He had absolute devotion to his family. He had a beautiful, shy smile and a twinkle in his eye that was completely captivating."

In 2003, George Gadson was commissioned to sculpt a bronze memorial bust of Pompey for permanent display in Delray Beach City Hall. The artist notes: "I wanted to convey a man with . . . great stature and tenacity . . . a kind and loving spirit who sought to assure equality for all." He adds: "The memorial is a tribute and testimony to his accomplishing goodwill amongst all he came in contact with . . ."

George Morikami Memorial

Address: Morikami Museum and Japanese Gardens, 4000 Morikami Park Road, Delray Beach. (561) 495–0233. Palm Beach County.

Morikami Museum and Japanese Gardens claims to be the nation's only museum dedicated exclusively to the living culture of Japan.

The Morikami memorial inside the two-hundred-acre park was a gift from the people of the Kyoto village of Miyazu in Japan, where George Morikami was born and raised. The memorial is a Japanese-style grave marker comprised of stone blocks piled to resemble a column.

Morikami's name and the family crest are inscribed on the memorial. His ashes are buried partly in a chamber near the bottom of the memorial and partly in Miyazu.

George Sukeji Morikami was born in 1887 and came to Delray Beach around 1906. Long-time Delray Beach resident Virginia Snyder knew him better than perhaps anyone. She was his friend and the administrator of his estate.

In 1967, while working as a newspaper reporter, Snyder learned about Morikami at a Palm Beach County Commission meeting she was covering for the *Fort Lauderdale News*. Intrigued, she located and interviewed him. A friendship evolved. What follows are her memories of him.

As a gesture of gratitude to an adopted community that had been good to him, Morikami wanted to donate about 150 acres of his land for use as a park. Located in western Palm Beach County, the land was undeveloped and largely unpopulated, so the commissioners rejected Morikami's offer.

Morikami twice offered his land to the City of Delray Beach and to the county's commissioners. Finally, the commission accepted. Today, the Morikami Museum and Japanese Gardens sits upon that land.

The story of George Morikami's migration to Delray Beach begins with Jo Sakai, a native of Miyazu who arrived in South Florida at the dawn of the twentieth century. Sakai

George Morikami Memorial, Morikami Museum and Japanese Gardens.

was in search of a site where he could set up a Japanese farming colony. He finally found suitable land in Palm Beach County, bought it and named his new enterprise Yamato Colony.

Sakai eventually went back to Japan to find men who would be willing to join Yamato Colony as pineapple farmers. Among those he recruited was George Morikami. The young man's motives for joining the colony were several.

"George was in love with a girl back in Japan," says Snyder. "Her family didn't approve of him because they were a samurai family and George was from a farming class. He thought that if he joined the Yamato Colony to learn modern methods of farming, it would impress her family."

Morikami never returned to Japan, although the Yamato Colony, an ambitious venture, failed because of a pineapple blight and because Cuban pineapples were underselling the colony's pineapples.

As time passed, Morikami bought parcels of land and grew pineapples and vegetables. By the late 1920s, he was wealthy. During the Great Depression, he lost his money. He became a vegetable broker. His fortunes again increased.

Morikami's life changed again after the Japanese attack on Pearl Harbor in December 1941. Many Japanese U.S. residents and citizens were put in internment camps, a fate that Morikami was spared because the fruits and vegetables he grew were valuable to the U.S. war effort. However, the local barber in Delray Beach refused to cut Morikami's hair, and the local feed store wouldn't sell feed to him. It was an isolating, troubling time, and Morikami sought solace from his land.

"George sometimes napped in his pineapple fields," says Snyder. "He turned on his tractor lights to work the fields at night. He dug out a lake and stocked it with fish. He took the dirt and formed it into what looked to him like Mount Fuji, a reminder of his homeland."

At the end of his life, George Morikami was stooped from decades of hard work but he was a gentle, peaceful man who loved the land he cultivated. His legacy is that land—a gift to the people of Delray Beach.

Visitors today come to Morikami Museum and Japanese Gardens to learn about Japanese culture, to enjoy Japanese festivals and demonstrations and to walk among the tranquil lakeside gardens, just as George Morikami envisioned.

Major William Lauderdale Memorial

Address: Forest Ridge, a residential community. Pine Island Road just south of SW Thirtieth Street, Davie. Broward County.

The memorial statue representing the supposed likeness of Major William Lauderdale is in a most unexpected location. It is inside the entrance to a Broward County residential enclave called Forest Ridge. This is not a gated community, so anyone can drive up to the statue.

Here, on a marble base rising from three 360–degree brick steps, looms the bronze figure of Major Lauderdale astride his horse. He hunches forward as though he is searching for Seminole warriors.

William Lauderdale was born into a Scots-Irish family in Virginia around 1782. When he was a teenager, he moved with his family to Sumner County, Tennessee. His father was a cotton and tobacco planter.

Indian raids in the area prompted the local militia to hold drills on the Lauderdale property, and it is likely that Lauderdale learned combat skills from observing these exercises.

After his father died, Lauderdale took over the plantation, and it prospered. Among the neighbors who befriended him was Andrew Jackson.

In 1812, Lauderdale was a captain in the Fifteenth Regiment of the Tennessee Volunteer Infantry, and Jackson was a major general (Tennessee Online 2005). With the Red Stick Creek tribes attacking Alabama settlements, Jackson, mending from a wound he had sustained in a duel, trusted Lauderdale to oversee the troops sent to quell the Creeks.

An interesting aside is that one of the Indians fleeing from Lauderdale and his Tennessee Volunteers was a young boy known to officers Jackson and Lauderdale as "Powell."

The Native American boy escaped to the swamplands of Florida and years later emerged as a Seminole warrior named Osceola (Tennessee Online 2005).

In 1823, at nearly forty years old, Lauderdale married his first wife, Polly. Together they had three children, but after only six years of marriage, Polly died. Lauderdale's second wife, Helen, bore him three more children.

Osceola rose up against the white man's treaties and the Indian Removal Act of 1830. The act called for the Seminoles to relocate to Arkansas. Amid the uprisings, President Jackson turned to Lauderdale and his Tennessee Volunteers.

In 1837, with the Second Seminole War in full force. Lauderdale, now a major, raised an army of five hundred Tennessee Volunteers to march into Florida.

Their mission was to find Seminole villages, and this they did, from Fort Jupiter south to the New River in Broward County, along a path or military trail that they cleared. After reaching the New River, they built a fort.

In March 1838, General Thomas Jessup issued an order directing that the fort should be named for Major Lauderdale. That same month, Lauderdale and his Volunteers fought the Seminoles on Pine Island. The battle was a victory for Lauderdale.

In April, he headed home to Tennessee. Suffering from a long-term lung ailment, he was too weak to walk on his own. On May 10, just one day before Lauderdale and his men were to be officially mustered out of service, he died in Baton Rouge, Louisiana, en route to Tennessee.

Lauderdale was buried in a cemetery in Baton Rouge, but no one today knows the location of his grave. Similarly, there is no known image of Major Lauderdale, which is why the memorial statue of him in Davie bears an imagined likeness.

Major William Lauderdale Memorial.

There are two bronze plaques on the memorial statue, one facing east and the other facing west. The west-facing plaque reads:

Pine Island was named by early explorers because it actually was an Everglade island before the area was drained for human habitation in the early 1900s. Formed thousands of years ago by the Atlantic Ocean tides, this 2½-mile-long anchor-shaped island rises 29 feet above sea level and is the highest natural point in Broward County.

. . . Among the earliest recorded inhabitants were the prehistoric Tequesta people of South Florida who had settlements here until their disappearance in the 1700s . . . . Later, various Seminole tribes established settlements here. . . .

The east-facing plaque reads:

William Lauderdale arrived in Fort Lauderdale with his combined brigade of Tennessee Volunteers and Regular Army volunteers on March 5, 1838. . . . Appointed by President Jackson, Lauderdale was sent to Florida to aid in fighting the Seminole War.

He selected a site on the New River for his fort. . . . Major Lauderdale's troops set out after the Indians and fought the last major skirmish of the war on this site on March 23, 1838.

The Indians and their chief, Sam Jones, escaped harm. However, their hasty retreat forced them to leave all their possessions behind, weakening their ability to survive in large groups.

One of Major Lauderdale's sons was killed during the Mexican War. Lauderdale County, Tennessee, is named for the major's brother James, who died in the Battle of New Orleans. Lauderdale himself remains somewhat of a mystery, a man without a face that people can see in textbooks or portraits.

Aside from the memorial statue in Davie, the only significant tribute to Major William Lauderdale is the city in South Florida that was named for him, and that city has placed him on the map of Florida history.

Brian Piccolo Park

Address: 9501 Sheridan Street, Cooper City. (954) 437–2600. Broward County.

Brian Piccolo, a football player for the Chicago Bears from 1966 to 1969, became a sports legend thanks to the 1971 TV movie *Brian's Song*, starring actors James Caan and Billy Dee Williams.

Located on 180 acres in western Broward County, Brian Piccolo Park is a memorial to a talented athlete who died before his time. Considering its namesake, the park befittingly focuses on sports.

It opened in 1989 as a sports complex offering football and soccer fields, cricket pitches, basketball, racquetball and tennis courts and a Velodrome.

A plaque on the wall of the park's administration building reads:

> Dedicated to the memory of Brian Piccolo, 1943–1970, who developed his athletic skills at an early age in the parks and playgrounds of Broward County and went on to become one of its most famous athletes. His life and his untimely death of cancer at age 26, has provided our youth with a legacy of athletic skill and personal courage.

Piccolo was born in Pittsfield, Massachusetts, but grew up in Fort Lauderdale. He moved there with his parents and two brothers when he was three.

At Central Catholic High School, he was an offensive tackle and later a halfback for the football team. He won a scholarship to Wake Forest University. In his freshman year in 1961, he scored five touchdowns. In his senior year, he scored seventeen touchdowns, notes a biography of Piccolo on the ESPN Web site (Puma).

In 1964, Piccolo signed with the Chicago Bears and became good friends with his Bears teammate, running back Gale Sayers. They became roommates, a historic event in that this was the first time that an African American NFL player and a white NFL player roomed together.

When Sayers suffered a serious knee injury in 1968, Piccolo helped him get through intensive rehab, and Sayers returned to the team the following year.

Entrance to Brian Piccolo Park.

About that time, Piccolo developed a lingering cough and chest pains. He went for a chest X-ray, which revealed a tumor on his lung. He underwent a biopsy that confirmed a malignancy.

Piccolo checked into Sloan Kettering Cancer Center in New York City. The diagnosis was grim: a large tumor in his chest cavity.

This was a rare form of cancer that had been lying dormant for perhaps all of Piccolo's life. The football star underwent a 4½-hour operation to remove the tumor. Afterward, he started chemotherapy. Through it all, he believed that he would go back to playing football, noted sportswriter Roy Taylor in his salute to Piccolo on the Chicago Bears History Web site.

Early the following year, Piccolo discovered another lump on his chest, so he went back to Sloan Kettering. Once again, he needed surgery. This time, it was more drastic, and Piccolo realized that he could never again play football. For someone who so loved the game, this news was devastating.

Surgeons removed Piccolo's left breast, some lymph nodes and his left lung. The cancer was so aggressive that nothing seemed to stop its destructive path. It spread to his liver.

On June 16, 1970, Brian Piccolo died, leaving his wife Joy and their three young daughters to mourn the loss of a man whom Gale Sayers described as having "the heart of a giant" (Puma).

Each year, the Chicago Bears team bestows the Brian Piccolo Award on a rookie or a veteran encompassing the same admirable traits that Piccolo possessed.

Carl Fisher Memorial

Address: Carl Fisher Park, Alton Road and Fifty-first Street, Miami Beach. Miami-Dade County.

He was called "the P. T. Barnum of the automobile age." Carl Graham Fisher was born in Indianapolis in 1874 and died in Miami Beach in 1939. His acumen and imagination helped turn Miami Beach into a Southern vacation capital.

The budding entrepreneur was ambitious. He opened a bicycle shop when he was a teenager. The automobile was in its infancy, but Fisher turned to selling cars.

He came up with the idea of making auto headlights. In partnership with two friends, he formed the Prest-O-Lite Company, which he later sold to Union Carbide. The sale made Fisher a multimillionaire (Burnett, Vol.1, 1986, 205).

Fisher believed that cars were the transportation mode of the future. He built the Indianapolis Motor Speedway in 1911. In 1915, he spearheaded the construction of the Lincoln Highway, connecting New York to San Francisco.

In the 1920s, Fisher built Dixie Highway, a 1,300–mile roadway linking Miami to Chicago, as well as Lincoln Road on Miami Beach, an upscale dining and shopping strip.

During Florida's land boom in the early 1920s, Fisher invested in Miami's beachfront property, which he then sold as lots. His promotion of the area as a tropical paradise caught the fancy, and the pocketbooks, of the wealthy.

But there also was room for middle-class tourists, who got into their cars and headed onto Fisher-built roads and highways for vacations in Miami Beach.

The words "It's June in Miami," which emanated from Fisher's huge lighted sign in Times Square, seduced New Yorkers seeking a respite from the winter weather (Miller).

The good that Carl Fisher did for Miami Beach was tainted by his anti-Semitism. His property deeds contained restrictions against Jews, and Fisher-developed hotels along Miami Beach bore signs that these hotels were for "Gentiles Only" (Burnett, Vol. 2, 1986, 238).

In the mid-1920s, the Land Bust, and then the Great Depression, washed over Miami Beach. Even after Fisher's

Carl Fisher Memorial, Carl Fisher Park.

empire crumbled in the debris of these events, some hotels continued the restrictive policy by advertising "No Jews, no dogs" or "Every room . . . without a Jew" (Burnett, Vol. 2, 1986, 238).

Carl Fisher was no "closet bigot," but ironically, by the late 1940s, and continuing today, Miami Beach had become a haven for Jewish retirees and vacationers whose religion made no difference to other hotel proprietors.

Carl Fisher's life ended in personal and financial ruin. He became a heavy drinker, and he and his wife Jane divorced. He had married her in 1909, when he was thirty-five. She was twenty years his junior.

Fisher's net worth was once reported at fifty million dollars. By 1939, the year he died, his fortune was long gone. He lived quietly and forgotten in Miami Beach.

Fisher's "if you build it, they will come" instincts had been right. Just as Ben "Bugsy" Siegel stood in the middle of a Nevada desert and foresaw the great gambling mecca of Las Vegas, Fisher had his own epiphany: a swampland morphing into a South Florida tourist mecca.

A granite memorial to Fisher is located in front of Fisher Park in Miami Beach. It includes a large bronze bust of the entrepreneur wearing a cap, eyeglasses and a smile. The words above the bust pay homage to a flawed visionary:

Carl Graham Fisher. He carved a great city from a jungle.

George Merrick Memorial

Address: 405 Biltmore Way, Coral Gables. Located in front of Coral Gables City Hall, facing LeJeune Road and Coral Way. Miami-Dade County.

A bronze statue of George Merrick stands on a six-foot-high coral-rock base in front of City Hall. It is a memorial to a visionary who in the 1920s transformed an expanse of farmland into the city of Coral Gables or, as Merrick defined it, the "City Beautiful."

The twelve-foot-tall statue captures Merrick looking out at his city. His right hand holds onto the suit jacket he has slung over his shoulder. In his left hand, he grasps rolled-up blueprints.

The statue was dedicated on May 23, 2006, as a gift to the city of Coral Gables from the Coral Gables Garden Club and donors.

George Merrick's father Solomon was born on the eastern shore of Maryland. While attending Lebanon Valley College in Ohio, he met a fellow student, Althea Fink, whom he married. Their son George was born in Springdale, Pennsylvania, in 1886.

Solomon earned a divinity degree from Yale University and became a Congregationalist minister at a church in New York. Then, he was called to minister at a church in Duxbury, Massachusetts.

Althea Fink Merrick was an artist and a teacher. Her father had become wealthy as a manufacturer of patent medicines. One of his salesmen praised Florida's great climate and opportunities, so Grandpa Fink convinced Solomon and Althea Merrick to start a new life there.

Solomon purchased 160 acres of Florida land on which he grew fruits and vegetables. George Merrick grew up in a small cabin on this property, which was about five miles from Miami and was the nucleus of what became Coral Gables.

Merrick quit school at age thirteen and worked alongside the field hands. The Merrick statue's sculpted hands resemble those of a manual laborer.

George Merrick Memorial.

George and his father turned the Merrick property into one of the area's largest grapefruit and vegetable plantations. Eventually, the site grew to 1,600 acres.

Arva Moore Parks, a local author and historian who is writing a book about Merrick, says he was well read. He attended Rollins College in Winter Park and New York Law School for one year.

He really wanted to be a writer, Parks says. He had already written poetry and fiction and had won a writing contest sponsored by a New York newspaper.

Merrick returned to South Florida in the summer of 1910 because his father was incapacitated by heart problems and needed him to take over the plantation. Solomon died in 1911.

George Merrick lived in the house, named Coral Gables, that Althea had designed and that Solomon had completed building in 1910.

The house is listed on the National Register of Historic Places and is open to the public as a tourist attraction. Not surprisingly, its most distinctive feature is its coral gables.

The house was built from limestone obtained from a nearby rock quarry. That quarry, now known as Venetian Pool, is listed on the National Register of Historic Places and is a major Coral Gables attraction.

Venetian Pool was designed by architect Phineas Paist and artist-illustrator Denman Fink, who was George Merrick's uncle. It features waterfalls, porticos, fountains, caves and grottos. Esther Williams once swam in its coral rock lagoon.

Merrick went into the real estate business in 1913. For the next five years, he developed subdivisions.

In 1916, Merrick married Eunice Peacock. Her family members were among the first settlers in Coconut Grove.

Merrick, now the owner of the plantation, envisioned developing it into a city mirroring the Mediterranean architecture of Italy and Spain.

His City Beautiful would have public fountains and archways, and upscale residential enclaves featuring beautiful homes with loggias, wrought-iron balconies and barrel-tile roofs. He would call his city Coral Gables, after the coral-colored gables on his family home.

Merrick was close to his uncle, Denman Fink, who was only six years his senior. Together with Denman, his cousin H. George Fink and landscape architect Frank Button, Merrick drew up plans and laid out the Coral Gables development. They sold their first lot in 1921.

Merrick took out an advertisement in the *Miami Metropolis* on November 16, 1921, extolling the virtues of his new planned city:

Coral Gables . . . the creation of beauty and the bringing true of dreams that will . . . endure and . . . age as does the everlasting coral upon which this master development is founded.

Parks describes Merrick as charismatic and likeable. At age twenty-eight, he became a Dade County commissioner. He donated one million dollars and 160 acres to the founding of the University of Miami.

Merrick had a financial interest in the magnificent Biltmore Hotel, in Coral Gables. He also loved tropical plants. For a time, he served as a director of Fairchild Tropical Gardens in Miami.

In the 1920s, Florida went through a land boom and then a land bust. The land bust depleted Merrick's fortune, and he fell on hard times. He opened a fish camp in the Florida Keys. In 1940, he became postmaster of Miami.

Merrick died in 1942. He was only fifty-six years old. He and Eunice are buried in Woodlawn Park Cemetery, in Miami's Little Havana neighborhood.

Parks says that before Eunice Merrick died in 1989, she expressed regrets that in the ensuing decades after her husband's death, he seemed to have been forgotten.

Eunice was a founder of the Coral Gables Garden Club. Betsy Adams, chairwoman of the club's George E. Merrick Monument, says that Eunice's concerns generated interest among the club's members, donors and the City of Coral Gables in placing the statue of Merrick in front of Coral Gables City Hall.

The statue would have pleased Eunice Merrick, for it ensures that George Merrick is not forgotten.

5

Southwest Florida

Fort Jefferson at Dry Tortugas National Park

Address: Dry Tortugas keys, in the Gulf of Mexico. Monroe County. Accessible only by seaplane or ferry.

People hear the name "Alcatraz" and they think of an impregnable fortress surrounded by shark-infested waters. In the 1800s, people thought of Florida's Fort Jefferson in a similar way.

Located nearly seventy miles west of Key West, in the warm waters of the Gulf of Mexico, Fort Jefferson is America's largest nineteenth-century coastal fort. The fort was built on eleven acres of Garden Key, one of seven small coral reef islands comprising the Dry Tortugas section of the Florida Keys. The Tortugas, along with their surrounding waters and shoals, constitute the one-hundred-square-mile area that is Dry Tortugas National Park.

The U.S. Army began construction of Fort Jefferson in 1846. It was built as a military fortress to protect U.S. coastal waters, particularly Mississippi River trade headed for Atlantic ports, notes an entry for Fort Jefferson in the *Columbia Encyclopedia* (Bridgewater and Kurtz 1968).

It took sixteen million handmade bricks to build Fort Jefferson. During the Civil War, the fort was occupied by Union forces. A moat wall surrounds the fort. When the fort's main wall was completed in 1862, it reached forty-five feet high, notes the National Park Service.

Fort Jefferson's most famous prisoner was Dr. Samuel Mudd, a Maryland physician and a Confederate sympa-

Fort Jefferson, Dry Tortugas National Park.

thizer. On April 15, 1865, Mudd set the broken left leg of President Lincoln's assassin, John Wilkes Booth.

Convicted of conspiring to kill the president, Mudd was sentenced to a life term at Fort Jefferson. Between soldiers, prisoners and civilians, there were about two thousand people at the fort at that time.

The fort's isolation, squalid living conditions, mosquitoes and heat must have been torturous for Mudd. However, those discomforts paled in comparison with the horrors of the yellow-fever outbreak that hit Fort Jefferson in 1867. Half of the fort's population, including Mudd, contracted the disease. As one officer's wife described the scene, "the whole island became one immense hospital. We seemed in some horrible nightmare" (Burnett, Vol. 3, 1986, 176).

After the garrison's surgeon died of yellow fever, Mudd volunteered to tend to the stricken, even though he was weak and ill himself. For this selfless act, President Andrew Johnson pardoned Mudd in 1869. The former prisoner returned home and continued to practice medicine. He died in 1883 at age fifty.

Partially hidden between two trees on Fort Jefferson's parade grounds, a beautiful stone memorial bears witness to the indiscriminate ravage of the 1867 yellow fever outbreak at Fort Jefferson. The Joseph Smith Monument reads:

In memory of Brevet Maj. Joseph Sim Smith, asst. surgeon
U.S. Army who died at this post of Yellow Fever Sept. 8,

1867 in the 30th year of his age. In admiration of his virtues as a man, of his zealous and impartial conduct as an officer and his devotion to his profession.

Companies L, M, I and K of the 5th Artillery have erected this monument . . . Henry Price, only son of Joseph Sim Smith, who died at this post of Yellow Fever Sept. 18, 1867, age 3 yrs. and 6 mos.

By 1875, the army had abandoned the fort. The Dry Tortugas became a wildlife refuge in 1908. In 1935, President Franklin D. Roosevelt designated it as Fort Jefferson National Monument. In 1992, it was rededicated as Dry Tortugas National Park.

The Dry Tortugas National Park ferry *Yankee Freedom II* is a high-speed catamaran that departs daily for roundtrip excursions from Key West. Historic Tours of America and Yankee Fleet operate the ferry. An onboard naturalist leads a guided tour of the fort.

Many passengers come for the tour and to enjoy the beach that overlooks Florida's most desolate fort.

Monument to Joseph Smith, Fort Jefferson, Dry Tortugas National Park.

Key West Historic Memorial Sculpture Garden

Address: Along the shoreline on Water (Wall) Street, Key West. Monroe County.

Sandy Cornish (1793–1869) was a freed slave who had been born in Maryland. He lost the papers that proved he had bought his freedom and when he was captured and faced with the inevitability of being sold at a slave market, he took desperate measures.

He mutilated his ankle and hip joints and cut off the fingers of one hand so he would be useless as a slave. His strategy worked; no slave owner would consider buying him. Cornish and his wife moved to Key West, and there, in spite of his self-inflicted injuries, he became a successful farmer.

The story of Key West pioneers like Sandy Cornish might be relegated to oblivion were it not for the Key West Historic Memorial Sculpture Garden, an extraordinary tribute in bronze to thirty-six men and women whose influence on the history of Key West is indelibly stamped.

Residents, businesses and a local group called Friends of Mallory Square raised funds to build the sculpture garden. It debuted in 1997.

That year, Friends of Mallory Square published the book *Key West Historic Memorial Sculpture Garden*, by Tom and Lynda Hambright, to spotlight the thirty-six busts and the garden's enormous bronze entrance sculpture.

Standing twenty-five feet high and eighteen feet long, *The Wreckers* pays tribute to the local nineteenth-century wreckers who salvaged cargo from shipwrecks along the reef. It was sculpted by Miami-based artist James Mastin.

Surrounded by wrought-iron gates, the brick-paved sculpture garden is a collection of thirty-six busts on individual pedestals, each bearing a plaque that gives a brief biography and describes the significance of the person whom the bust memorializes.

The history of Key West is incomplete without acknowledging the importance of the wrecking industry to the city's economy.

Bust of Sandy Cornish, Key West Historic Memorial Sculpture Garden.

Among the busts is that of John Bartlum (1814–1871), a wrecker and a shipbuilder who came to Key West from the Bahamas. He built a ten-ton sloop, *Mary McIntosh*, as well as several schooners and a 950–ton clipper ship, the *Stephen R. Mallory*.

The sculpture garden also displays a bust of William Curry (1821–1896), who owned a Key West wrecking company and ship's chandlery. His holdings were vast and varied, and he is touted as Florida's first self-made millionaire.

Cigar manufacturing was a vital industry in early Key West history. Accordingly, the garden features a bust of Eduardo H. Gato (1847–1926). A native of Cuba, Gato ran the largest cigar factory in Key West.

Several busts pay tribute to women such as Ellen Russell Mallory (1790–1855), a native of Ireland who moved to Key West in 1823. She worked as a nurse and ran a boarding house. Her son Stephen was secretary of the navy for the Confederacy. There is a bust of him, too.

Lena Johnson (1870–1932) earned a living in Key West by baking cakes and making taffy. She taught her craft to local girls and became a member of the city council, a political position that no woman had previously held.

There is a bust of John Lowe, Jr. (1833–1917), who owned a local sponge business and a lumberyard. The sponging industry was another commercial force in Key West in the mid-1800s.

Twentieth-century Key West is represented by the bust of Joe Pearlman (1892–1980), a Romanian-born businessman who arrived at the tip of Florida in 1904. Civic-minded and philanthropic, he was a real-estate developer and a long-time president of B'nai Zion, a synagogue in Key West.

From doctors, lawyers and politicians to ship captains, judges, Ernest Hemingway and Harry S. Truman, the Key West Memorial Sculpture Garden embodies the spirits of thirty-six men and women who had a profound impact upon Key West.

Key West-Florida Keys Historical Military Memorial

Address: Mallory Square, Key West. Monroe County.

Beneath a flagpole flying the American flag in Mallory Square, ten stone and bronze pedestals, each providing information about the military presence in Key West, comprise the Key West-Florida Keys Historical Military Memorial.

The pedestals commemorate Key West's involvement in campaigns and wars spanning three centuries, including the Civil War, the Cuban Missile Crisis, the Mariel Boat Lift and the present-day war on drugs.

Key West-Florida Keys Historical Military Memorial.

At the end of the pedestals rests a ten-inch forward-gun turret that was salvaged from the USS *Maine*.

The Second Seminole War pedestal explains how and where Seminole tribes attacked white settlers in the Keys. To protect citizens from further attacks, the frigate *Constellation* arrived in Key West in 1836.

The Civil War pedestal describes how a U.S. Army captain marched his troops from the northeast side of Key West to its southwestern shore, which thwarted Confederate sympathizers from taking over the city.

By 1862, nine hundred Union soldiers were in Key West, and two hundred more were stationed in the Dry Tortugas at Fort Jefferson, including the New York and Pennsylvania Volunteer regiments and the Second U.S. Colored Infantry Regiment. There hundreds of army and navy personnel died from yellow fever epidemics during the war.

The Spanish American War pedestal chronicles naval events after the battleship USS *Maine* sailed from Key West to Havana in 1898.

The ship sank in Havana's harbor after being destroyed in an unexplained explosion on February 15, 1898. Wounded crewmen were transported to Key West, where the city's customhouse hosted a court of inquiry into the sinking of the *Maine*. The ship's destruction precipitated the Spanish-American War. According to the World War I pedestal, Key West was a major naval training base. In 1914, the Key West Naval Station became headquarters for the Seventh Naval District, the overall command for naval forces in Florida.

The World War II pedestal covers the function of destroyers and seaplanes operating from Key West and explains how the naval base supported naval operations in the Caribbean. The U.S. Navy created a fleet sonar school in Key West, and the local airport was under the navy's control.

The Cold War pedestal gives insight into the importance and power of the U.S. Navy's operations in Key West during a period of strained relations between the United States and the former Soviet Union.

Key West became the largest anti-submarine warfare training and development center on the East Coast. A rear admiral commanded the naval base, which had a submarine squadron and a destroyer division.

There were so many navy personnel stationed in Key West, they outnumbered the city's nonmilitary residents.

The Cuban Missile Crisis pedestal covers events during 1962, when U.S. military troops and aircraft arrived in Key West, naval ships left the harbor and the military protected the island's shoreline after President Kennedy declared a naval and air quarantine of Cuba.

The "War on Drugs" pedestal relays how patrol aircraft and patrol boats stationed at Key West hampered the illicit importation of marijuana. The monument also highlights how U.S. Armed Forces and nonmilitary drug enforcement agencies are combating illegal seaborne shipments of cocaine.

From Key West's colorful Duval Street and its museums and attractions, to its beautiful Victorian bed-and-breakfast inns, the island is a magnet for visitors. However, its playful atmosphere tends to overshadow an important fact to which the Key West–Florida Keys Historical Military Memorial pays tribute:

For three hundred years, Key West has played a vital role in Florida's military history.

Ernest Hemingway Memorial

Address: In front of the Key West Museum of Art and History at the Custom House, 281 Front Street (at Whitehead), Key West. (305) 295–6616. Monroe County.

Key West has been home to many important authors, but no literary figure has left a more indelible mark on the island than did Ernest Hemingway.

Hemingway's decade-long residency in Key West is memorialized in a six-foot-tall bronze sculpture created by artist Terry Jones. It is on permanent display in front of the Custom House.

The sculpture was dedicated on July 21, 2005, the 106th anniversary of Hemingway's birth. It depicts Hemingway in his thirties, looking as he did when he lived in Key West. He is wearing a cap and carrying a fishing rod. (Hemingway's love for fishing was legendary.)

In 1928, Hemingway and his second wife Pauline arrived in Key West to pick up a new Model A Ford that was a gift from her uncle, Gus Pfeiffer.

When the couple walked into the local dealership, the Trevor and Morris Company at 314 Simonton Street, they were apologetically informed that the car hadn't arrived.

To pacify an irritated Hemingway, the dealership offered to put them up in an apartment over the dealership's garage until the car arrived. It was in that apartment that Hemingway wrote the draft to *A Farewell to Arms*. (Sandler 1996, 240).

He had already written several books, one of which, the acclaimed novel *The Sun Also Rises*, had made him a cause celèbre in Paris where he and Pauline had been living. In Key West, nobody had heard of him.

In 1931, the Hemingways decided to make Key West their home. They paid eight thousand dollars for a big, run-down Spanish colonial house at 907 Whitehead Street that had been built in 1851. While workmen whipped the structure into shape, Hemingway wrote *Death in the Afternoon*, a nonfiction work about bullfighting (McIver 1993, 24).

Today visitors to Key West can take a guided tour of the

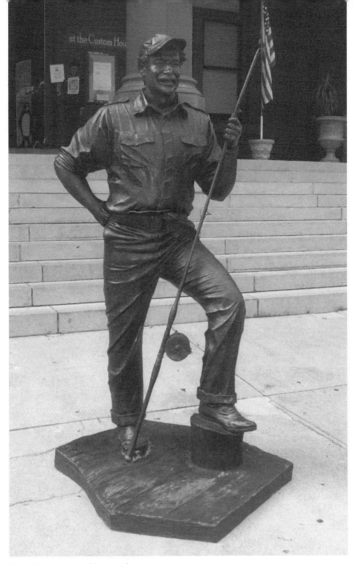

Ernest Hemingway Memorial.

Hemingway house to learn much more about the author's life, his manuscripts, his drinking and fishing escapades, the friendships he made and his famous six-toed cats, whose descendents roam the property today.

There is the story of the in-ground swimming pool that Pauline installed in 1937 as a surprise for her husband, who was in Spain covering the civil war there.

When Hemingway returned home, he was so angry that Pauline had paid twenty thousand dollars to build the pool that he pulled a penny from his pocket, threw it on the ground and told her she might as well have taken his last cent (McIver 1993, 27–28).

One of Hemingway's closest friends in Key West was Joe Russell, who owned a fishing boat and a speakeasy that we now know as Sloppy Joe's. Fishing and drinking were high-priority pastimes for Hemingway, so perhaps it's not surprising that the two men were friends.

While Hemingway lived in Key West, he wrote prolifically, including the novel *For Whom the Bell Tolls*, the nonfiction work *The Green Hills of Africa* and the short story "The Snows of Kilimanjaro."

In 1953, Hemingway won a Pulitzer Prize for his novel *The Old Man and the Sea*. In 1954, he won the Nobel Prize for Literature. He committed suicide in 1961.

Today, visitors can take a walking tour tracing the novelist's footsteps through Key West. The annual Hemingway Days Festival, held in July, includes a Hemingway lookalike contest. The Key West Museum of Art and History displays Hemingway-related artifacts.

These and other activities comprise Key West's diverse tribute to one of America's greatest authors.

Florida Keys Memorial (1935 Hurricane Monument)

Address: MM 81.5, U.S. 1 in Islamorada, on Matecumbe Key. Monroe County.

The Labor Day Hurricane of 1935 was the worst disaster in the history of the Florida Keys. Today, cable TV's The Weather Channel ranks it the most powerful hurricane of the twentieth century. What made it the "Storm of the Century"?

On the evening of September 2, 1935, sustained winds of at least 160 miles per hour and a twenty-foot-high storm surge claimed more than four hundred lives on Matecumbe Key and in Islamorada (*Palm Beach Post*, August 25, 2007).

The victims included many of the approximately 650 World War I veterans doing road construction to extend the Overseas Highway linking Miami to Key West. Other victims included visitors and residents.

In the early years of the Great Depression, many Americans were out of jobs and going hungry. President Franklin

Florida Keys Memorial (1935 Hurricane Monument).

D. Roosevelt created the Federal Emergency Relief Administration (FERA) to provide work programs.

Why did the hurricane claim the lives of so many World War I veterans? Because under the FERA program, these veterans flocked to Matecumbe Key and lived in work camps while doing the road construction.

There are many horror stories about what happened to Matecumbe Key residents during the hurricane. Seventeen-year-old Bernard Russell survived, as did his father, but not before Bernard thought he would surely be killed. "Killer in the Keys," an article by Jeff Klinkenberg published in the *St. Petersburg Times*, recounts Bernard Russell's ordeal (*St. Petersburg Times*, August 14, 1991).

When his family home flooded, he sought safer shelter, but the angry winds blew a flying object into his back and knocked him down, and at one point, the waters nearly covered his face. Through blinding rain, Russell made his way to a railroad car and hid there.

The hurricane demolished Russell's house and blew away about thirty members of his family, including his mother and sister and his infant cousin. Bernard Russell eventually married Laurette Pinder, a local girl who had survived the hurricane.

Members of the Russell family are buried in Pioneer Cemetery on the grounds of the luxurious Cheeca Lodge, a resort located near the Florida Keys Memorial. The Matecumbe United Methodist Church owns the cemetery, where Matecumbe Keys' early settlers are buried.

These settlers include the Russells, who began homesteading in 1854, and the Pinders, who homesteaded in 1873. The Labor Day Hurricane demolished the local church, the schoolhouse and beachfront homes.

The Florida Keys Memorial, also known as the 1935 Hurricane Monument, was created in 1937 and is listed on the National Register of Historic Places.

The plaque on the memorial is inscribed:

Dedicated to the memory of the civilians and war veterans whose lives were lost in the hurricane of September 2, 1935.

The memorial base is made of stone and concrete. Five steps lead to a crypt holding the remains of about three hundred civilians and veterans who died from the hurricane's fury. A ceramic tile map of Key Largo to Marathon Key is carved in the top of the crypt.

Looming above the crypt, an eighteen-foot-tall stone monument features a bas relief—a low-raised sculpture—depicting palm trees savagely blowing as they are slammed by a tidal wave.

The Federal Arts Project (FAP), administered by the Works Progress Administration (WPA), was created in 1935 during the Depression to provide jobs for unemployed artists.

Under this project, sculptor Lambert Bermelman and several other professional artists contributed their artistry to this memorial. The site is a somber reminder that Mother Nature has two faces: beautiful and ugly.

Lawrence "Jungle Larry" Tetzlaff Memorial

Address: Naples Zoo at Caribbean Gardens, 1590 Goodlette-Frank Road, Naples. (239) 262–5409. Collier County.

Lawrence "Jungle Larry" Tetzlaff and his wife, Nancy "Safari Jane," turned Naples' Caribbean Gardens into Collier County's major attraction, Naples Zoo at Caribbean Gardens, after they bought the property and opened it to visitors in 1969.

"My father loved animals but he was good with people, too," says Tim Tetzlaff, Larry and Nancy Jane's youngest son. "He knew how to talk to them rather than down to them. He genuinely loved animals and people."

The biggest experts on Jungle Larry's life are his sons Tim and David, and these are Tim's recollections of his father.

Larry Tetzlaff was born and raised in Kalamazoo, Michigan. He was fascinated with snakes and collected and cared for them. Wild-animal collector Frank Buck offered Tetzlaff a job as a reptile keeper at the 1939 World's Fair.

From there, 6' 6" Larry found a job as a stuntman for Johnny Weissmuller in the 1939 movie *Tarzan Finds a Son*, which was shot on location at Silver Springs.

During World War II, Larry was hired by a pharmaceutical company to milk venomous snakes to extract their venom, which could be used as an antidote or as an anticoagulant.

When the war ended, Larry went back to the Midwest and started a collection of wild animals that he brought into schools in Michigan, Pennsylvania and Ohio. He gave educational presentations that delivered a conservation message and explained the value of these animals.

At a small Ohio theme park called Puritas Springs, Larry maintained an exhibition area for his extraordinary animals, one of which was a cougar. The cougar took a strong liking to a young animal-lover named Nancy Jane, who gave skating lessons at the theme park and who often stopped by to visit Larry's animals. In 1957, she became Mrs. Lawrence Tetzlaff.

Lawrence "Jungle Larry" Tetzlaff Memorial. Photo courtesy of Tim Tetzlaff.

In spite of her love for animals, Nancy Jane was terrified of snakes. She knew that the only way to overcome her fear was to face it head on. She told Larry to put a boa constrictor around her shoulders and to keep it there until she stopped screaming. The plan worked.

The Tetzlaffs traveled around the world to promote conservation and to find animals to bring back to zoos. They filmed their encounters.

In 1964, Larry and Nancy Jane started a zoo at Ohio's Cedar Point theme park, and as successful as it was, they wanted to find a winter home in a warm climate so their animals could be outside year round.

During a vacation in Florida in 1967, the Tetzlaffs visited Naples. There they discovered Fleischmann's Caribbean Gardens and knew this would be the perfect place for their zoo.

In the early 1900s, the property had been owned by botanist and conservationist Henry Nehrling. His garden boasted three thousand species of tropical plants. Julius Fleischmann, of the Fleischmann's yeast family, bought, restored and improved Nehrling's garden and filled it with tropical birds.

When Fleischmann died in 1968, Larry and Nancy Jane bought the fifty-two-acre property, then called Caribbean

Gardens. The Tetzlaffs moved to Florida with their two young sons and their animals and renamed the site Naples Zoo at Caribbean Gardens.

The zoo claims to be the only one in Florida with Indochine tigers and all four of Africa's top predators: lions, spotted hyenas, leopards and African wild dogs.

While Jungle Larry worked with many kinds of animals, he had an affinity for the big cats. He trusted his knowledge of these animals. He also trusted his instinct.

On one occasion, a full audience at Naples Zoo watched as a cougar joined Larry in the arena. Larry took note of the cougar's body language and halted the performance when he sensed that the cat was in an uncooperative mood. The audience was vocally disappointed.

That day in the audience there happened to be a circus animal trainer who understood why Larry had stopped the show. The trainer told the audience, "This is one of the smartest men I've seen. That cat is going to do something dangerous."

Jungle Larry died after a short illness in 1984. His son Tim notes that Larry was "a showman and a man who tried to show people the importance of conservation and the beauty and importance of wild animals."

As a tribute to Jungle Larry, Tim and David created a memorial comprised of a granite stone on a wooden stand, forty-eight inches high by fifty-four inches wide. It is located next to the zoo's Backyard Wildlife Habitat. The memorial is inscribed:

> In loving memory of "Jungle" Larry. Colonel Lawrence Tetzlaff. He will always love people and animals.
>
> Outstanding showman, animal trainer, TV star, author, lecturer, motion picture producer, herpetologist, double for Tarzan, expedition leader to Australia, South America and Africa . . . conservationist, member of the Explorer's Club, former president of Florida Attractions Association and Governor's Wildlife Committee for Florida.

J. N. "Ding" Darling Memorial

Address: J. N. "Ding" Darling National Wildlife Refuge, 1 Wildlife Drive, Sanibel. (239) 472–1100. Lee County.

Renowned cartoonist Jay Norwood "Ding" Darling died in 1962 at age eighty-six and was buried in Sioux City, Iowa. In 1967, Sanibel National Wildlife Refuge was renamed in his honor. He was, after all, passionate about wildlife conservation.

Darling was born in Michigan in 1876. By age twenty-four, he was cartooning for the *Sioux City Journal*. By 1906, he was drawing political cartoons for the *Des Moines Register*. He signed his cartoons "Ding," a combination of his first initial and the last three letters of his last name, notes a U.S. Fish and Wildlife Service biography of the artist.

An active outdoorsman, Darling was aware of the vulnerability of wildlife species and habitats, so his cartoons focused on everything from the plight of ducks searching for flyways to humanity's disregard for natural habitats.

Darling was a two-time Pulitzer Prize-winner for his cartoons. Focusing on political, social and economic issues, he drew about fifteen thousand editorial cartoons that appeared in more than one hundred newspapers.

In 1934, President Franklin D. Roosevelt appointed Darling director of the U.S. Biological Survey, a precursor to the U.S. Fish and Wildlife Service.

Darling helped pass the Migratory Bird Hunting Stamp Act, which requires waterfowl hunters' licenses to bear a federal duck stamp. Proceeds from the sale of the stamp go to wetlands purchase and preservation.

The cartoonist designed the first federal duck stamp, which depicted a mallard drake and a hen in a wetland. He later designed the blue goose symbol that became the logo for the National Wildlife Refuge system.

In 1984, the U.S. Postal Service issued a fiftieth-anniversary commemorative reprint of the Darling-designed federal duck stamp and sold more than 100 million of them, notes the J. N. "Ding" Darling Foundation.

J. N. "Ding" Darling Memorial, J. N. "Ding" Darling National Wildlife Refuge. Photo by Dennis Souers.

J. N. "Ding" Darling National Wildlife Refuge, totaling about 6,300 acres, is home to more than two hundred bird species. It is a pristine landscape of sea-grass beds, mangrove islands, hardwood hammocks and open water.

There is a memorial bust of Darling at the park's visitor center. It was donated by the sculptor and by the J. N. "Ding" Darling Foundation. The bronze bust has the following inscription:

J. N. "Ding" Darling. 1876–1962. Renowned cartoonist and pioneering conservationist, Darling's many lasting contributions to the conservation of our nation's natural resources include the establishment of this National Wildlife Refuge. Artist Bruce B. Everly Sr.

At the bottom of the visitor center ramp, a stone monument is inscribed:

J. N. "Ding" Darling was a renowned cartoonist and ecologist whose perceptive mind, eloquent pen, and skilled brush endeared him to newspaper readers and conservationists during a long career and a lifetime of ecological concern.

Ding's syndicated cartoons . . . often dealt with waterfowl and the conservation of natural resources.

He was one of the earliest supporters of the Migratory Bird Hunting Stamp program. . . . He designed the First Federal Duck Stamp and the familiar National Wildlife Refuge flying Canada goose sign.

For many years, Darling had a winter home on Captiva Island. He initiated . . . the establishment of the Sanibel National Wildlife Refuge, renamed in his memory in 1967.

It was Darling's hope that future generations could share the beauty, serenity, and the bounty of nature he had known.

"Sgt. Clayton" Memorial

Address: Centennial Park, 2100 Edwards Drive, Fort Myers.
(239) 332–287. Lee County.

The African American soldier stands before a wall within
a gate. The gate symbolically leads to freedom from slavery, and the bronze life-size soldier memorializes African
Americans who served during the Civil War.

This memorial to the Second Regiment of U.S. Colored
Troops (USCT) is known as the Sgt. Clayton Memorial.
Sculptor D. J. Wilkins says he chose the name because it
took a "ton of clay" to sculpt the statue, notes the Beaches of
Fort Myers/Sanibel Web site.

Specifically, the statue commemorates the black Union
soldiers who defended a federal post in Fort Myers against
the Confederates.

Fort Harvie had been built in 1841 as a military defense
post during the Second Seminole War. It was rebuilt for use
during the Third Seminole War.

Its name was changed to Fort Myers at the direction
of Major General David Twiggs, the commander of Fort
Brooke, which is now Tampa, according to Downtown Fort
Myers.com.

Twiggs chose the name to honor his future son-in-law,
Colonel Abraham C. Myers, the son of the head rabbi of
Charleston, South Carolina. Colonel Myers had fought in
the Mexican War and served as chief quartermaster of the
War Department of Florida (Southwest Florida Pioneers
Historical Society 2002).

Fort Myers was cattle country and a major supplier of
beef for the Confederacy. It was there, in February 1865,
that the southernmost battle of the Civil War took place as
Confederate and Union forces, including the USCT, fought
each other for six hours.

Of about 200,000 Union soldiers who were African
American—a group comprised of Northern freedmen, former slaves and escaped slaves serving in about 160 "colored"
regiments—it has been estimated that 36,000 were casualties of the Civil War, notes Dick Weeks.

The USCT fought in more than four hundred engagements, and by war's end, thirteen black soldiers had been awarded the Congressional Medal of Honor, notes Kim Gaines in the article "Soldiers of Glory."

The plaque at the Sgt. Clayton statue reads:

> This memorial is dedicated to the 2nd Regiment Infantry, USCT and Companies D and I, which served at the Battle of Fort Myers. . . .
>
> On February 20, 1865, Confederates of the 1st Battalion Florida Special Cavalry attacked Fort Myers. The attack erupted into a cannon duel with the 2nd USCT in charge of artillery. . . . The Confederate forces withdrew. . . .
>
> The Battle of Fort Myers marked the final action of the 2nd USCT in South Florida. Companies D and I left Fort Myers in March of 1865. Fort Myers was then decommissioned. U.S. Colored Troops freed and enlisted over 1,000 of the enslaved in Florida during the Civil War.

In 2000, 135 years after the Battle of Fort Myers, sculptor D. J. Wilkins' statue of Sgt. Clayton was installed in Centennial Park as a tribute to the gallantry of the U.S. Colored Troops.

"Sgt. Clayton" Memorial.

Herbert Hoover Dike Monument

Address: Hoover Dike Road at Lake Okeechobee, off U.S. 27 (Sugarland Highway), Clewiston, Hendry County. 863–983–7979

"Okeechobee" is a Seminole word for "big water," an apt description of Lake Okeechobee. That body of water is the largest freshwater lake in Florida and the second largest freshwater lake in the continental United States.

Lake Okeechobee is a popular fishing spot because of its abundance of largemouth bass and it attracts nature lovers because its southern and western shores are bounded by wetlands that are a habitat for birds, fish and wildlife.

In Clewiston, on Lake Okeechobee Scenic Trail at the top of the Herbert Hoover Dike, the following words are inscribed in a plaque embedded in a stone monument:

> Started in 1932. Completed in 1938. Herbert Hoover Dike. During the 1926 and 1928 hurricanes, 2,500 lives were lost in the Lake Okeechobee area due to inadequate flood control. Hoover personally supported and was directly responsible for early Federal construction of Lake Okeechobee levees for protection of life and property.
>
> By act of Congress, July 14, 1960, Lake Okeechobee levees were designated Herbert Hoover Dike in commemoration of Herbert Hoover's humanitarian efforts and interest in public safety, which permitted the safe development of the rich potential of this region.
>
> Constructed by Jacksonville District Corps of Engineers, U.S. Army in cooperation with the State of Florida. Dedicated January 12, 1961. Hoover was here for the dedication.

"Lake O Dike Safe in Storm, Corps Says" ran the May 5, 2006, headline of the *Palm Beach Post*.

Journalist Robert King's article reported that a panel of state-commissioned engineers had inspected Hoover Dike, found weaknesses in it and expressed serious concern about its potential soundness during a hurricane.

For days, the newspaper ran articles about concerns about Lake Okeechobee. "Emergency Planners Ask for Federal Money for Dike," a May 9 headline declared.

Herbert Hoover Dike Monument.

Then-governor Jeb Bush recommended that the U.S. Army Corps of Engineers make daily inspections of the dike, strengthen it, speed up repairs to the levee and lower the lake's water levels during hurricane season.

In light of the alarming report, emergency planners began grappling with how to evacuate thousands of residents living in the vicinity of the dike should it fail during a hurricane

In a follow-up article on May 11, King quoted Colonel Robert Carpenter, who was head of the Army Corps of Engineers' Florida operations. Carpenter called the report a "careless choice of words," and assured residents around the dike that they were safe.

Carpenter assured the public that the Corps was continuing to repair and stabilize the 143-mile-long, 300-foot-wide dike and that his staff would address the report's suggestions.

The impacts of hurricanes Frances and Jeanne in September 2004 were still on the minds of residents living around Lake Okeechobee. Even more vivid were memories of Hurricane Wilma's damage to homes and streets in Broward and Palm Beach counties in October 2005.

The possibility of additional hurricane damage during the summer of 2006 made locals uneasy, especially as Tropical Storm Ernesto threatened to reach hurricane force.

Ernesto was more bark than bite. The storm did little more than dump heavy rain on Palm Beach County. Hurricane season arrived and departed in silence.

Lake Okeechobee is serene and beautiful, but for people living in the vicinity of Hoover Dike, there is an uncertainty. What about next year?

Ironically, by August 2007, record-low water levels in Lake Okeechobee had dried once-saturated parts of the earthen dike and its underlying muck soils, as the *Palm Beach Post* reported on August 10, 2007.

According to the article, members of the South Florida Water Management District (SFWMD) feared that because of the low levels, dried parts of the dike could actually worsen leaks when the lake finally returned to a normal level.

The district had another concern, the article noted. Water at sites outside the lake could press into the dike. That scenario had occurred in 1974, causing a levee north of the lake to collapse in reverse.

The SFWMD reminded the U.S. Army Corps of Engineers that sudden water surges from future rains into the dried lakebed could create stress on floodgates or on culverts. The district asked the corps to inspect the stability of the dike. The corps was already planning to do this.

As the summer of 2007 ended, South Florida residents were hopeful that the hurricane season would be uneventful; however, they were aware that if a hurricane did hit, it would have one benefit. It would ease the lake's drought and give renewed meaning to the word "Okeechobee"—Big Water.

RAF Cadets Monument

Address: Civic Center Park, 100 Sugarland Highway, Clewiston. Hendry County.

In a park across from the historic Clewiston Inn, an American flag and a Union Jack fly above a stone monument. A plaque on the monument is inscribed with these words:

> Riddle Field, Clewiston. Between September 1941 and September 1945, 1,325 British cadets and 109 American cadets were trained and graduated as pilots. The 32 British cadets who were killed during training lie in the British Plot in an Arcadia cemetery. Now remembered each year by the people of that city.

RAF Cadets Monument.

A second plaque is inscribed:

This plaque is erected on behalf of those RAF [Royal Air Force] pilots who were trained nearby at Riddle Field, Clewiston between 1941 and 1945 and records their deep appreciation of the warm and generous friendship so frequently given to them by the people of Clewiston and of the state of Florida.

In a rural-agricultural Southern landscape that was Clewiston in the early 1940s, culture shock must have confronted the young British cadets who lived there while they were flight school students.

If the cadets were homesick, they must have appreciated the hospitality of the Clewiston community, which welcomed them. Many residents extended dinner invitations to the pilots.

In an article about British soldiers' experiences in Clewiston (*Palm Beach Post*, May 30, 2006), writer Eliot Kleinberg revealed how a dinner invitation changed the course of one Brit's life.

In December 1942, four months after British officer Tom Chappell came to Clewiston to train Royal Air Force pilots, he was invited for dinner at the home of a local family.

That's where Chappell met the hostess' sister, Julia. Romance blossomed. He and Julia were married the following June.

When Chappell's assignment was completed, he took Julia back to England, but within two years, they returned to Florida. That was more than sixty years ago.

Chappell is one of many British expatriates who attend memorial services conducted annually at the British plot at Oak Ridge Cemetery in Arcadia.

Thanks to the friendship that the people of Clewiston extended to Tom Chappell, he found a permanent home and six decades of memories in Florida.

Ponce de León Monument

Address: Gilchrist Park, 400 W. Retta Esplanade, Punta Gorda. (941) 575–3324. Charlotte County.

If you could stay young forever simply by drinking from a fountain, would you?

Legends say that explorer and conquistador Ponce de León discovered Florida while searching for a fountain of youth, a miraculous spring that would restore youth to those who drank from it.

For de León, finding the fountain was another reason for exploration, his primary reasons being his search for riches and colonization.

Every American has learned that in 1492, with the financial backing of King Ferdinand and Queen Isabella, Christopher Columbus set sail from Spain to explore new trade routes and new lands, and that his three ships were the Niña, the Pinta and the Santa María.

But fewer Americans know much about his second voyage to the Americas and its connection to Ponce de León.

De León is believed to have been born circa 1450 in San Servos, León, Spain. Trained as a soldier, he served in military campaigns against the Moors and accompanied Columbus on Columbus' second voyage to the Americas in 1493.

Columbus explored Hispaniola in the Caribbean, the eastern part of which we know as the Dominican Republic. He returned to Spain, but Ponce de León remained in the Caribbean and became deputy governor of Hispaniola.

In 1508, de León explored the island of Boriquen, taking possession of its gold, slaves and land and becoming governor. Because of the riches he found there, he renamed the island Puerto Rico.

The Carib natives supposedly told de León tales of a magical fountain whose waters could restore youth. De León was determined to find it. Around 1512, with authorization from Charles V to discover and colonize Bimini, in the Bahamas, he set sail for Bimini.

Ponce de León Monument.

In 1513, de León landed in the area of St. Augustine, Florida, and claimed the land for Spain. He named the land La Florida because his arrival coincided with the time of the Easter feast, Pascua Florida.

An interesting aside: In a most undeserving location, the parking lot of a motel at 137 San Marco Avenue in historic St. Augustine, there is a massive live oak tree called Old Senator.

At first glance, the branches are so long that you may think you are looking at two or more trees close together.

The Old Senator's beautiful branches spread so wide that you must cross to the opposite side of San Marco Avenue and stand back to view the entire tree.

What makes the tree so amazing is that it is estimated to be more than six hundred years old and is believed to have been there when Ponce de León set foot on the shores of St. Augustine.

Ponce de León continued to explore Florida by sailing along the coast and down to the Florida Keys. He came across an island populated with turtles and containing no natural fresh water supply, so he named the island Dry Tortugas.

De León returned to Spain. The king sanctioned a new voyage for de León, this time to colonize La Florida in the name of Spain. In 1521, de León took two ships and two hundred settlers and set sail for Florida (Bridgwater and Kurtz 1968).

He landed in southwestern Florida in an area believed to have been Charlotte Harbor. This was Calusa territory. The hostile Calusa warriors attacked the expedition.

There are conflicting reports about whether the Calusa arrow that hit de León pierced his stomach or his thigh, but whatever its location, the wound was serious. The Spanish colony disbanded and, with Ponce de León, sailed for Cuba.

The explorer's wound turned from serious to fatal. He died in Cuba at the estimated age of sixty-one, never having found a Fountain of Youth. He reportedly was buried in the Cathedral of St. John, in San Juan, Puerto Rico, where his tomb and his nearby house are tourist attractions.

Today in Gilchrist Park, in Punta Gorda, stands a fourteen-foot-high monument to Ponce de León. It consists of a life-size, castbronze statue standing on an eight-foot-tall white stone base.

The statue depicts de León wearing his plumed helmet and armor, a sword at his left side, his right hand raised and extended. The base inscription reads:

> The Royal Order of Ponce de León Conquistadors is an organization dedicated to the preservation of the Spanish heritage of Florida and especially Charlotte County. This bronze statue is of Juan Ponce de León who discovered Florida and Charlotte Harbor in 1513, returned in 1521 and attempted to establish a colony.

Every year in Punta Gorda, the Royal Order of Ponce de León Conquistadors stages a reenactment of the conquistador's landing at Charlotte Harbor.

In one form or another, Florida has memorialized the name Juan Ponce de León many times, from Ponce de León Boulevard in Coral Gables and De Leon Springs State Park to Leon County in the Panhandle and Ponce Inlet Lighthouse in Volusia County.

6

Central West Florida

The British Plot

Address: Oak Ridge Cemetery, North Lee Avenue and Livingston Street, Arcadia. De Soto County.

During World War II, hundreds of British Royal Air Force (RAF) cadets trained in Florida.

With German war planes invading England's skies, these cadets had to go elsewhere for their training and so, with Florida's welcoming arms and good year-round weather, they came to private flying schools in Arcadia, Clewiston and Lakeland.

In the southwest corner of Arcadia's Oak Ridge Cemetery, a Union Jack flies above a series of small granite headstones. This section of the cemetery is known as the British Plot. A memorial erected by the Rotary Club of Arcadia in 1968 explains why:

> Buried herein are 23 RAF cadets who died while in training at U.S. flying training fields in South Florida during World War II.

The plot is surrounded by a granite border engraved as follows:

> Commonwealth War Graves. Erected by a citizen of a grateful republic they died to save.

Among the headstones are those of Lionel Viggers, RAF, who was killed on October 4, 1944, when his plane was struck by lightning, and RAF trainees Roger Crosskey and Alfred Lloyd, who died in separate flying accidents in

The British Plot, Oak Ridge Cemetery.

1942. Some of the RAF cadets buried here were as young as nineteen.

Within the British Plot is the grave of "John Paul Riddle, MBE, 1901–1989. American pioneer of aviation. Co-owner of the flying school where the British cadets were trained during World War II." Riddle was a founder of Embry-Riddle, the aeronautics school in Daytona Beach.

On Memorial Day each year, a graveside service is held for the RAF cadets interred in the British Plot. For more than fifty years, Arcadia's Rotary Club has officiated at this event.

During the ceremonies, someone reads aloud the names of each deceased cadet, and people in the crowd come forward to place a wreath or a flower at each grave. Attendees sing "God Bless America" and "God Save the Queen."

Typically among these attendees are people who moved to Florida from Great Britain and who place a flower or a wreath on a grave and salute the Union Jack flying overhead.

Writer Eliot Kleinberg profiled this annual event in his article "Over Here, Brits Remembered" (*Palm Beach Post*, May 30, 2006). Kleinberg quotes the Commonwealth War Graves Commission's secretary-general, Bradley Hall, who spoke to the hundreds of people attending the ceremony that weekend.

Hall said that the annual services "honor those who made the ultimate sacrifice, and the cooperation of our countries in facing challenging times."

The British Plot seems anomalous in Arcadia, a town where cattle auctions are common, where local ranchers wear ten-gallon hats and where everyone has heard stories about Florida's whip-cracking "cracker" cowboys.

Yet, here, on a parcel of hallowed ground, brave young Brits continue to be remembered and honored.

A monument to the British and American pilots who trained at Riddle Field in Clewiston is located at Civic Center Park in Clewiston, in Hendry County.

Gunther Gebel-Williams Memorial

Address: Across from 1927 Train Station, 303 E. Venice Avenue, Venice. (941) 412–0151. Sarasota County.

In 1960, Ringling Bros. and Barnum & Bailey Circus made Venice, Florida, its headquarters. Venice's heyday as a winter circus capital is gone, but the town contains traces left by "The Greatest Show on Earth."

Near the train station that once transported performers, equipment and animals in Ringling Bros. and Barnum & Bailey Circus, a statue stands in memory of lion tamer and animal trainer Gunther Gebel-Williams.

Sculpted by Ed Kasprowicz of Apollo Beach, the eight-foot-tall bronze statue rests on a stone base whose plaque is inscribed, simply: "Gunther Gebel-Williams, 1934–2001."

The statue depicts Gebel-Williams grinning and wearing his familiar flowing cape. His open vest exposes his muscular chest. His blonde hair is long. His right hand extends dramatically into the air.

He was born Gunther Gebel in Schweidnitz, now Swidnica, in Poland. When he was twelve, his mother became a seamstress for the Circus Williams. The boy fell in love with everything associated with circuses.

Owner Harry Williams became Gebel's mentor and teacher, and the boy absorbed every aspect of circus life, from acrobatics to animal training. After Harry Williams' death, Gunther became the head of Circus Williams and adopted Williams' last name.

In 1968, Irvin Feld, owner of Ringling Bros. and Barnum & Bailey Circus, convinced the animal trainer to headline "The Greatest Show on Earth." However, to secure a commitment from Gebel-Williams, Feld had to pay two million dollars to buy the Circus Williams, notes the Ringling Web site.

One year later, Gebel-Williams made his American debut in the 109th edition of the Greatest Show on Earth, in Venice, Florida

The public crowned him with the nickname "Lord of the Ring." He had great rapport with animals, whether he was

Gunther Gebel-Williams Memorial.

working with tigers, leopards, lions, horses or elephants. "You can't tame tigers, you only train them," he once said (*St. Petersburg Times* obituary, July 20, 2001).

It took Gebel-Williams years to perfect his spectacular stunt of riding on a Bengal tiger as it stands on an Indian elephant's back. This feat was one of many that made him one of the world's highest-paid and most recognizable circus performers.

His induction into the Madison Square Garden Walk of Fame and his appearances on the *The Tonight Show Starring Johnny Carson* and in a CBS-TV special titled *Lord of the Rings* added to that recognition. He became known as "The Greatest Animal Trainer of All Time" and he had the scars to prove it.

Gebel-Williams became a household name after he filmed an American Express commercial in which he draped a leopard around his shoulders. He was a showman in the sense that he loved his animals, he loved his audiences, and they loved him in return.

Gebel-Williams' last performance was in Grand Rapids, Michigan, in 1998 when he stepped in for his son Mark Oliver, also an animal trainer. Gebel-Williams and his wife Sigrid retired to their home in Venice.

In 2000, Gebel-Williams was diagnosed with a brain tumor. In spite of surgery and aggressive treatment, he succumbed to cancer the following year.

To honor this much-admired circus entertainer, Ringling Bros. and Barnum & Bailey created the Gunther Gebel-Williams Foundation, based in Falls Church, Virginia.

According to a press release issued by Ringling Bros. on July 19, 2001, the foundation memorializes Gebel-Williams' "commitment to the partnership between humans and animals."

The press release quotes these words from Gebel-Williams' friend Kenneth Feld: "Gunther knew the mind of the animal and he taught us all to love and respect all living things. He set a standard for performing which will be almost impossible to match. The world has lost a true legend . . . a true hero."

West Venice Avenue Monuments

Address: W. Venice Avenue, Venice. Sarasota County.

The easiest way to find monuments dedicated to the city of Venice's past is to follow West Venice Avenue toward the Gulf of Mexico.

West Venice Avenue stretches through a placid neighborhood lined with shade trees and manicured old homes. A long, wide, grassy median divides the avenue's north and south sides. One memorial and two monuments are spaced along this median.

The Venice Army Air Base Memorial is about 100 feet east of a cozy lodging establishment called Inn on the Beach (725 W. Venice Avenue), located across from the gulf.

The Venice Army Air Base Memorial consists of two white stone columns joined by a white stone arch or bridge bearing the words "Venice Army Air Base." The arch is a one-third-scale re-creation of the original main entrance to the Venice Army Air Base.

Bronze plaques on the memorial's columns commemorate base personnel and present a history of the base.

Venice Army Air Base Memorial.

In 1942, U.S. Army surveyors arrived in Venice to scout for a suitable site on which to build a training facility for rear-echelon maintenance and service groups.

After the Venice Army Airfield opened in December 1942, maintenance crews trained there, and German POWs performed work assignments there. When World War II ended, the airfield became Venice Municipal Airport.

About twenty thousand servicemen trained at the base, including the all-Chinese Fourteenth Service Group, formed at the request of Madame Chiang Kai-shek.

According to one plaque, the base's original U.S. Army personnel were the Thirty-seventh Service Squadron of the Twenty-seventh Service Group:

> Followed by . . . HQ Squadron, 90th Service Squadron, 826th QM Co., 1728th and 1729th Ordnance COs, 1063rd Signal Co. and 1095 QM Co. . . . . First combat aircraft arrived from the 13th Fighter Squadron, 53rd Fighter Group for pilot training on June 7, 1943. The 14th Fighter Squadron soon followed. Pilot training began with the P-39, followed by the P-40, P-47 and finally the famous P-57 Mustang Fighters."

About 100 feet east of the Venice Army Air Base Memorial lies the Calusa and Seminole Peoples Monument, which pays tribute to both peoples. The bronze face of early Seminole chief Billy Bowlegs (Holata Micco) appears above a commemorative plaque. A bronze figure of a Calusa tribesman is to the left of the plaque. A bronze figure of a Seminole appears to the right.

East of this monument, a Pioneer Court Monument honors Venice's nineteenth-century settlers.

Three small bronze sculptures on the brick monument depict a man in front of an orange tree, a man with a cow and a man holding his fishing net. These images represent the pioneers' three main sources of food.

Beneath the sculptures, a bronze plaque describes the daily life and hardships experienced by the nineteenth-century pioneers, as well as their need for community support and socialization.

As the plaque explains:

Life was hard and beset by isolation and heavy physical labor, but companionship, climate and pioneer spirit combined to offer . . . contentment.

The words apply to nearly every long-ago settler who staked his or her claim to plots of land around Florida. In spite of attacks by indigenous tribes, voracious mosquitoes and a sometimes-inhospitable climate, the settlers persevered to build new lives for themselves.

John Ringling Memorial

Address: St. Armand's Circle, Sarasota. Sarasota County.

It was "The Greatest Show on Earth." The taste of the peanuts, the roar of the lions, the daredevil routines of the aerialists and the words of the ringmaster were all part of the excitement of the Ringling Bros. and Barnum & Bailey Circus.

On the corner of John Ringling Boulevard and Boulevard of the Presidents, in Lido Key, stands a statue of John Ringling dressed in a suit and tie. Sculpted by Tony Lopez, the dapper bronze figure holds a cane and hat.

The statue deliberately faces St. Armand's Circle and the Circus Ring of Fame. It is dedicated to the Seventy-fifth anniversary of St. Armand's Key, one of Sarasota's islands. St. Armand's Key is synonymous with Ringling.

John Ringling was born in Iowa in 1866; with his brothers he founded a family circus in 1884. In 1907, they bought the Barnum & Bailey Circus. Transporting the circus by train, John Ringling was able to expose Americans from coast to coast to the thrills of the circus.

The business made Ringling rich. His investments spanned dozens of businesses, including Madison Square Garden in New York City.

Ringling's wealth enabled him to buy and develop land in the Sarasota area during the 1920s. According to local lore, he used his circus elephants to transport construction materials to build a bridge from St. Armand's Key to the mainland.

Local lore also says that Ringling built St. Armand's Circle so his wife Mable, whom he married in 1905, wouldn't have to travel to Palm Beach to do her shopping. Tony boutiques and fine restaurants line St. Armand's Circle.

Through the years, John and Mable traveled the world, searching for new acts for his circus and buying priceless furnishings, tapestries and artwork for their Venetian Gothic mansion, which they named Cà d'Zan (House of John). Here, guided tours reveal aspects of Ringling's life.

John Ringling Memorial.

Completed in 1926, the mansion is among Sarasota's awe-inspiring Ringling-related tourist attractions. It measures two hundred feet long and has thirty-two rooms, fifteen baths and an eight-thousand-square-foot marble terrace with a commanding view of Sarasota Bay.

The mansion's facade is decorated with glazed, multi-toned terracotta, and the roof's barrel tiles were imported from Barcelona. A sixty-foot-high tower crowns the mansion.

Circus Ring of Fame.

John Ringling himself epitomized elegance, from his expensive Cuban cigars to his private-label whiskey, so it is not surprising that his home resembles a palace. According to Ringling Bros.' history, he spent about $1.5 million to build a spectacular home featuring magnificent ceiling murals painted with cherubs and dancing figures. Nor is it surprising that John and Mable were collectors of fine art, especially works by Baroque masters such as Rubens, Van Dyck and Velasquez. Some of these paintings are huge enough to cover entire walls in museums.

In fact, they do. Today, the John and Mable Ringling Museum of Art in Sarasota, the state art museum of Florida, is home to the Ringlings' collection of paintings and objets d'art. The art museum is part of a sixty-six-acre estate that includes Cà d'Zan and the Ringling Circus Museum.

1929 was a devastating year for Ringling. Mable died. The stock market crashed. Ringling's fortunes diminished, and he had health problems. He died in 1936.

The Circus Ring of Fame, encircling a small park on St. Armand's Circle, is one more tribute, although indirectly, to John Ringling. It consists of in-ground brass plaques that pay tribute to famous circus performers. A circus wagon wheel is etched into each plaque.

Probably the most famous of these performers was Emmett Kelley, who created the tramp clown character Weary Willie. There also is a plaque dedicated to Josephine Berosini, an aerialist who danced and balanced on a bicycle seat on the high wire while she was blindfolded.

Another performer memorialized with a plaque is animal trainer Mabel Stark, the first woman to train tigers. Wrestling a tiger was her trademark routine.

John Ringling, more than anyone, transformed Sarasota into a breadbasket of culture and entertainment.

Joan M. Durante Community Park

Address: 5550 Gulf of Mexico Drive, Longboat Key. (941) 316–1988. Manatee County.

Longboat Key is a twelve-mile-long ribbon of high-end condos, vacation rentals and private homes surrounded by the Gulf of Mexico and Sarasota Bay.

When attorney James Durante retired as partner with the law firm of Fulbright and Jaworski, he and his wife, Joan, moved permanently from New York City to Longboat Key, where they had previously spent winter vacations.

The following are James Durante's memories of his wife. Consider his tale a love story.

Joan and James Durante first met when she became his secretary. Although of Norwegian stock, she had reddish-brown hair and what James Durante describes as "large, bright brown eyes."

"Her beauty was self-evident," he says. "She had an opportunity to become a professional model but she wasn't interested."

Durante says that not only was Joan beautiful, she also was a loving wife who always wanted to please him. He doesn't recall their ever having a serious argument.

Joan became active in developing Longboat Key's community theater. An amateur artist, she also became involved with the local art center.

In 1989, Joan was stricken with food poisoning. She was in the hospital for a month, sometimes seeming better, and sometimes getting worse.

To this day, neither the doctors nor James Durante knows how Joan contracted the food poisoning from which she died in 1990 at age fifty-nine. "Thirty-six years of a happy marriage ended," he says.

The local art center's main pavilion is named for Joan Durante, but James Durante wanted to honor his wife's memory in a way that would benefit the entire community.

Durante entered into an agreement with the town. He offered what he says eventually totaled one million dollars to restore an odd piece of land the town owned and to develop

Visitors strolling in Joan M. Durante Community Park.

it into a community park. The town, he says, eventually extended the land from twenty-four acres to thirty-two acres.

The property initially looked like an overgrown swampland to Durante, but by the time the Joan M. Durante Community Park opened in 1994, it had emerged into a beautiful wetland and coastal hammock forest with a mix of wildlife and plants surrounding a pond with a fountain in the center.

The walking paths are dotted with golden rain trees, silver buttonwoods, periwinkles, orange milkweed, roses, sunflowers, jacaranda, hibiscus and bougainvillea. From November to Easter, the park hosts Sunday concerts.

At the entrance to the park, there is a memorial that states:

> May all who enter these hallowed grounds be embraced by love, tranquility, beauty, contentment and goodwill. Those are the qualities that brightly marked the life of Joan M. Durante.
>
> James P. Durante. 1992.

Durante says many people have told him how much they enjoy the park. That pleases him because the park does bring beauty and contentment into their lives, just as Joan M. Durante brought beauty and contentment into her husband's life.

As he says, "The park is a living memorial to my wife."

De Soto National Memorial

Address: 3000 NW Seventy-fifth Street, Bradenton. (941) 792–0458. http://nps.gov/deso. Manatee County.

At the De Soto National Memorial, which commemorates the explorer's landing on Florida soil, the story of Hernando de Soto's journey through Florida and westward to the Mississippi River unfolds. A park ranger, interpretive panels and a short film aid the story.

One thing is certain: Spanish conquistador Hernando de Soto was cruel, even ruthless, toward Native Americans he encountered during his expedition through Florida in 1539.

Conquering peoples for financial gain was something de Soto learned at an early age. He joined Francisco Pizarro's forces in overthrowing the Incas in Peru. He returned to Spain to live a rich man's life but he was seduced by tales of gold and treasures in the New World.

De Soto convinced Charles V to let him explore and colonize the New World in the name of Spain. Equipped with more than six hundred soldiers, priests, several women and other followers, as well as pigs, war dogs and more than two hundred horses, de Soto sailed for the New World.

He landed on Florida's west coast on May 30, 1539. Wearing swords, helmets and armor, de Soto's army must have appeared formidable as they rode on horseback into the local villages. Some of the native people were friendly. Others weren't.

The greedy conquistador took their chieftains hostage and threatened to kill them if the Indians refused to reveal where their gold and treasures were located. Often, the Indians claimed that treasures lay in the next village.

Along the memorial site's nature trail, an interpretive sign quotes de Soto's letter to the Spanish magistrate in Cuba, dated July 9, 1539. De Soto wrote: "They say there are many trades among the Indians, abundance of gold and silver, and many pearls. . . . Of what the Indians say, I believe nothing but what I see, although they know . . . if they lie to me it will cost them their lives."

Holy Eucharist Monument, De Soto National Memorial.

De Soto enslaved many of the Native Americans and forced them to carry his soldiers' belongings as they marched across uncharted territory. He chained these captives to make certain they would not try to escape.

Thousands of Native Americans died at the merciless hands of the army, from being torn apart by de Soto's dogs or from being exposed to disease, but in the end, de Soto didn't fare well, either.

Despite his lengthy travels through Florida and southeastern and southwestern states and across the Mississippi

River in search of gold, silver and jewels, de Soto came away empty handed.

De Soto's dreams of glory died with him after he succumbed to a fever in 1542. His soldiers buried his body in the Mississippi River.

The Holy Eucharist Monument and Memorial are located along the park's nature trail. In 1995, The Catholic Diocese of Venice erected the sixty-foot-high cross in memory of the twelve priests and friars who accompanied de Soto's expedition and in dedication to all priests who serve in Florida.

The diocese also owns the Holy Eucharist Monument, a limestone monument about twenty-five feet high with a carved stone base. The monument is also known as the Hernando de Soto National Memorial.

Judah P. Benjamin Confederate Memorial at Gamble Plantation State Historic Site

Address: 3708 Patten Avenue, Ellenton. (941) 723–4536. Manatee County.

The magnificent mansion at Gamble plantation still stands, the only remaining antebellum plantation home in south Florida.

A park ranger and interpretive panels and exhibits chronicle the history of this site. The entire plantation site is considered a memorial to Benjamin.

Supported by seventeen of the original eighteen columns and bearing outer walls almost two feet thick, the two-story ten-room mansion was slave-built between 1844 and 1850. Fifteen years after its completion, a famous Confederate cabinet member would seek refuge here as he fled a federal warrant.

Judah P. Benjamin Confederate Memorial, Gamble Plantation State Historic Site.

In the 1840s, Robert Gamble moved from Leon County to Manatee County, where he started a sugarcane mill on the Manatee River. At the height of his plantation's success, Gamble owned 3,450 acres and 300 slaves.

However, Gamble's fortunes changed and by 1856 he was so deeply in debt that he was forced to sell his plantation and sugar-mill operation to two Louisiana planters, who paid him $190,000.

During the Civil War, Union sailors on a blockade schooner sailed by Gamble plantation. Mistakenly convinced that Confederate president Jefferson Davis owned the site, the sailors burned the sugar mill. For whatever reason, they left the mansion intact.

In the early 1870s, the property came into the hands of George Patten in exchange for his paying three thousand dollars in back taxes. The property was too costly to maintain, so the Patten family sold off chunks of the land. The mansion eventually fell into disrepair.

In 1925, the Judah P. Benjamin Chapter of the United Daughters of the Confederacy (UDC) bought the sixteen-acre property and deeded it to the State of Florida as a historic site.

The Patten House, an onsite farmhouse built circa 1895 by George Patten's son, serves as a museum and the Florida headquarters and the Judah P. Benjamin Chapter of the UDC.

Park rangers at Gamble plantation explain to visitors that this is a memorial site because Judah P. Benjamin, Confederate secretary of state, hid there while fleeing federal forces at the end of the Civil War.

Indeed, an upstairs bedroom, exhibiting a large photo of Benjamin, is practically a shrine to him. This is the room he occupied while hiding at the mansion.

It was from the balcony outside this room that Benjamin could see whether federal troops had discovered his whereabouts and were about to arrest him.

Judah P. Benjamin's life was a study in melodrama. He was born on the island of St. Thomas in 1811. When he was ten, he moved with his Sephardic parents and his siblings to Charleston, South Carolina.

As author Eli N. Evans describes in his biography of Benjamin, Charleston had five hundred Jewish residents by 1800, the largest Jewish community in the nation. Charleston was tolerant toward Jews, and Benjamin did not have to downplay his religious beliefs.

His religion became a major issue only in his adulthood, when the repeated sting of anti-Semitic comments led him away from the Jewish traditions and practices he had previously observed. He was compelled to keep a low religious profile.

Benjamin studied law at Yale University and practiced law in New Orleans. As a lawyer, he helped form the Illinois Central Railroad. He owned a sugar plantation and 140 slaves, but sold the plantation and the slaves in 1850.

Benjamin married a Creole woman, Natalie St. Martin. He indulged and spoiled her, but there were whispers of her infidelities. She separated from him and went to live in Europe with their young daughter Ninette.

In 1852, Benjamin became a U.S. senator from Louisiana, the first *acknowledged* Jewish U.S. senator. (David Levy Yulee, who became U.S. senator from Florida in 1845, was Florida's and the nation's first Jewish-born U.S. senator, but he turned his back on his religion.) In addition to being admired for his brilliant mind, Benjamin gained a reputation as a great orator.

During one Senate debate, he took offense at what he considered an anti-Semitic remark from a fellow senator. Benjamin is said to have made the following retort:

> It is true that I am a Jew, and when my ancestors were receiving their Ten Commandments from the immediate Deity, amidst the thunderings and lightnings of Mount Sinai, the ancestors of my opponent were herding swine in the forest of Great Britain. (Evans, 1988, 97)

Confederate president Jefferson Davis appointed Benjamin Confederate secretary of war and then as secretary of state. For up to twelve hours a day, Benjamin worked alongside President Davis.

According to Evans' biography of Benjamin, Davis' wife, Varina, described Benjamin as her husband's loyal and trusted "right hand." In her later years, she wrote that Benjamin's "greatness was hard to measure" and added that she "loved him dearly" (Evans, 1988, 216).

When the Civil War ended, Benjamin, fearing capture and aided by sympathizers, made his way from Richmond to Florida, sometimes wearing disguises.

From Gamble plantation, Benjamin headed south to flee the country. A pink granite monument in Sarasota commemorates an important juncture in his clandestine voyage. Measuring about five feet tall and inscribed with two crossed Confederate flags, the monument stands near the corner of Tenth Street and U.S. 41 (Tamiami Trail) in Sarasota. It reads:

> Near this spot on June 23, 1865, Judah P. Benjamin, Secretary of State for the Confederacy, set sail for a foreign land.

With the help of blockade runner Captain Frederick Tresca, Benjamin sailed to Nassau, Bahamas, and Havana, Cuba, before setting off to England, where he was warmly received. There he became a respected and successful barrister.

His "Treatise on the Law of Sale of Personal Property," which he wrote in 1868, is still referred to by British law students.

Benjamin reunited with his wife and daughter when he retired to Paris. He was buried in a Paris cemetery in the Boursignac family plot, the name of his daughter's in-laws. His gravestone reads:

> Judah Philip Benjamin. Born St. Thomas, West Indies, August 6, 1811. Died in Paris May 6, 1884. United States Senator from Louisiana. Attorney General, Secretary of War and Secretary of State of the Confederate States of America. Queens Counsel, London.

Andrews Memorial Chapel

Address: 1899 San Mateo Drive, Dunedin. (727) 529–9233. Pinellas County.

In 1868, Reverend Joseph Brown arrived in Dunedin from Rockbridge County, Virginia, to minister to the town's small number of Presbyterian settlers, many of whom were of Irish-Scottish descent.

In fact, some Dunedin streets, such as Highland Avenue and Scotland Street, pay tribute to that ancestry. Likewise, the town's name harks back to Scottish legends and literature, which refer to the city of Edinburgh as "Dunedin."

At the Dunedin Historical Society and at Andrews Memorial Chapel, visitors can learn about the chapel's history, particularly the tragedy that led to its name.

For three years, the Presbyterian congregation held worship services in a log schoolhouse. In the spring of 1871, they

Andrews Memorial Chapel.

held a meeting in which they agreed to organize a church, Bethesda Presbyterian Church.

According to Dunedin Historical Society's director, Vincent Luisi, in 1876, twenty-five-year-old William Andrews was caught in a storm while returning to his Dunedin home after visiting his fiancée. Lightning spooked Andrews' horse.

The violent storm uprooted a tree and tipped it over, killing Andrews in its path. The young man's father, a local cattle rancher named John G. Andrews, was grief-stricken over the sudden death of his son. He wanted to memorialize William in some way.

It happened that at the time John Andrews' Presbyterian congregation was preparing to build a church, so he decided to make them an offer they couldn't refuse.

Two congregants donated the land for the church, and thus began the building of a wooden house of worship made from local and non-local timber and with nails that came from a foundry in Richmond, Virginia.

The cost of building the church was high, and this fact wasn't lost on the congregation, so John G. Andrews found a way to pay homage to his deceased son while doing something beneficial for his church.

He offered to donate two hundred dollars toward the construction costs, but with the stipulation that the church be named in memory of his son, William. The congregation agreed.

It took two years until completion, but by the end of 1878, Rev. Joseph Brown was conducting services at the new church, Andrews Memorial Church.

By 1888, the congregation had grown, and it became evident that they needed a larger church building. That year, the original chapel was dismantled and used for parts throughout the community of Dunedin.

Newly built Andrews Memorial Church, a white, picket-fenced Victorian structure, made its debut at a different location from the original church that had been taken apart.

By 1970, this church building was showing signs of deterioration. To prevent it from being torn down, the Dunedin Historical Society raised money to transport the building to its present address at the entrance to Hammock Park. The church is still surrounded by a white picket fence.

Now known as Andrews Memorial Chapel, the restored building is listed on the National Register of Historic Places.

The sanctuary ceiling is made from heart pine. The chapel features two foyers with Gothic archways. The pews are seventeen feet long, and the stained glass windows are original.

The chapel is generally open to the public on Sundays from 2 p.m. to 4 p.m. and continues to serve as a memorial to a young man who, more than 130 years ago, was in the wrong place at the wrong time.

Sponge Diver Memorials

Address: Sponge docks on W. Dodecanese Boulevard, Tarpon Springs. (727) 937–6109. Pinellas County.

The fishing village of Tarpon Springs in northwest Pinellas County is the next best thing to actually going to Greece. Nicknamed the "Sponge Capital of the World," Tarpon Springs has been steeped in Greek history and culture since the late 1800s. It is a city full of ethnic pride.

In the 1880s, Philadelphian John K. Cheyney was marketing Tarpon Springs as a winter resort when he realized that the gulf waters there, rich with sponge beds, could yield a mighty harvest that would spawn a lucrative industry. He started a wholesale sponge business (Tarpon Springs Chamber of Commerce).

In 1895, John Corcoris immigrated to America from his native Greece where for generations his family had been involved in the sponge business.

When Corcoris arrived in Tarpon Springs and explored the Gulf of Mexico, he found thick, prime-quality sponge beds immersed in the deeper waters. He was convinced that the best way to get to those beds was by deep diving.

At the time, the customary method of sponge fishing in the United States was to go out in a boat and plunge a hooked pole into the waters to retrieve sponges closer to the surface (Burnett 1986, 70).

Corcoris bought a fishing boat and a standard diving suit, the kind with an air hose and a metal helmet fronted by a glass face-piece. This was what sponge divers wore in Greece to dive deep enough to reach the sponge beds.

John Cheney and John Corcoris formed a business relationship, and Corcoris brought his brothers from Greece to Tarpon Springs. Hundreds of other Greek divers followed.

Among those who are familiar with the town's sponge-diving past is George Billiris, born in Tarpon Springs in 1927. A historian with ties to the sponge industry, George traces his local ancestry to John Billiris, who left Greece in 1904 and came to Tarpon Springs to become part of the

Sponge Diver Memorial, Tarpon Springs sponge docks.

sponge industry. For many Tarpon Springs residents of
Greek heritage, this is a familiar story.

As described by George Billiris, Tarpon Springs' Hellenic atmosphere grew in the early 1900s as people from the
Greek islands carved their traditions into the Florida town,
turning it into a Greek coastal village.

Billiris can tell you that Tarpon Springs is a city of traditions: fishing boats laden with sponges, divers diving for

sponges, Greek pastries forming tantalizing bakery displays and worshippers attending services at St. Nicholas Greek Orthodox Cathedral.

The aroma of Greek foods wafts from restaurants, and during the annual Feast of the Epiphany, Greek boys dive into Spring Bayou in hopes of retrieving the golden cross and being blessed by the archbishop.

Another Tarpon Springs tradition centers on the sponge auctions formerly held at the sponge docks. Divers brought up the sponges, boats hauled them in, the sponges were cleaned, bleached and trimmed, and sponge brokers bid on the sponges. Tourists still peruse the bins and boxes of sponges for sale.

According to the town's chamber of commerce, in the 1930s, there were about two hundred boats bringing in 3 million dollars' worth of sponges to Tarpon Springs' docks. In the 1940s, a bacteria called Red Tide destroyed most of the sponge industry in Tarpon Springs; however, in recent times, new healthy beds have grown. Divers still go down into the waters to bring up sponges, but today they wear wetsuits and diving masks.

Tarpon Springs' sponge industry may not be as large as it once was, but it continues. Today visitors can take a boat ride from the sponge docks to view sponge-diving exhibitions.

In addition to attracting sponge divers from the Greek islands, Tarpon Springs became home to generations of Greek chefs. Many of the immigrants who came to Tarpon Springs opened restaurants, permeating salty air with the aromas of authentic Greek cuisine. Visitors today can still find those delicious flavors at restaurants like Mykonos and Mama's Greek Restaurant.

Until recently, one of Tarpon Springs' most visited Greek restaurants was that run by Louis Pappas, on 10 Dodecanese Boulevard. It has since closed. In front of the building, there is a bronze statue of a sponge diver and a plaque with this inscription:

A tribute to sponge divers of Tarpon Springs, Florida. At the turn of the century, divers from the 12 Grecian Isles settled here to establish a sponge industry. In his memory, the family of Louis M. Pappas commemorates in his perpetual honor this courageous diver.

The whole of Tarpon Springs seems to pay tribute to the sponge industry. Here and there, you'll find markers, bronze plaques and memorials to the divers who, because of the nature of their work, often put themselves in harm's way.

In an article on one of the Tarpon Springs diving statues (*Suncoast News*, April 24, 2002), reporter Mark S. Schantz pointed out that diving is not without risks.

These risks include divers getting the "bends" if they stay too long in the water or come up too fast, and divers' boats catching fire and burning.

Another bronze statue of a diver stands with his back to the river along the sponge docks. The young diver holds a helmet in his hands.

A gift from members of the local community, the statue honors the courageous and skilled sponge divers who built an industry and brought Greece to Florida.

José Martí Memorial

Address: Parque Amigos de José Martí, 1303 E. Eighth Avenue, Ybor City, Tampa. (813) 247–6323. Hillsborough County.

Nineteenth-century Cuban poet, essayist and orator José Martí's fervent wish was for his native Cuba to be liberated from Spain's rule.

What more likely place for Martí to deliver his imploring speeches than Ybor City? These speeches were meant to raise funds to support insurgents willing to fight for Cuba's independence, and in the 1890s, there was a large Cuban population in Ybor City.

Known as America's Cigar Capital because of its numerous cigar factories, the Tampa neighborhood of Ybor City was named for Cuban-born Vicente de Ybor, who owned a large cigar factory there.

Ybor's factory and Ybor City itself were melting pots of Italian, Hispanic, black and even Jewish cigar workers. They worked and lived harmoniously in Ybor City. They built thriving social clubs, such as the Italian Club, the Cherokee Club and Centro Español (the Spanish Club).

José Martí Memorial, Ybor City. Photo courtesy of Bob Leonard.

José Martí Memorial, Key West.

Between 1891–1895, José Martí visited Tampa about twenty times. Ybor City's Cuban patriots and Martí's friends offered their homes to him during his visits. At least once, he stayed at the Cherokee Club, notes the Ybor City State Museum.

Many times Afro-Cuban patriot Paula Pedroso and her husband Ruperto, a cigar worker, hosted Marti at their modest boarding house. In 1893, Marti took refuge there after an assassination attempt on his life.

That year, thanks to Martí's impassioned speeches, including one he delivered from the steps of Ybor Square, the cigar workers raised one million dollars to help finance a revolution against Spain.

Martí also delivered his heartfelt message of freedom to Cubans living in Key West, and there, in Bayview Park on Truman Avenue and Eisenhower Drive, stands a bronze memorial statue honoring Cuba's beloved patriot.

In Tampa, one memorial stands out because of its ties to pre-Castro Cuba. The memorial is located on parkland partially paid for with contributions from the Cuban government under Fulgencio Batista, who was ousted by Fidel Castro's guerilla movement in 1959.

The diminutive Parque Amigos de José Martí (Marti Park) was built on the site where the Pedrosos' boarding house once stood.

Inside the park gates, the statue of Martí depicts him with his right hand extended, as though he is pleading for support to free his beloved Cuba. Originally bronze, the statue is painted white, a nod to the white marble statues of Martí that proliferate in Cuba. The park is managed by the Cuban Historical and Cultural Center.

Spurred by José Martí, the War of Independence began in Cuba on February 24, 1895. It launched simultaneously in four locations, including Guantanamo. The popular song "Guantanamera" is based on "Simple Verses," one of Marti's poems, according to the CasaCuba web site.

Three months after the revolution started, Martí was killed during a skirmish with Spanish soldiers. He was forty-two years old.

A new Cuban government was elected in 1897, but the War of Independence continued long afterward. In Cuba, February 24 is celebrated as a national holiday, and José Martí is regarded as the father of the country, a martyr who died fighting for a free Cuba.

At the end of the short-lived Spanish-American War in 1898, Spain relinquished its hold on Cuba. This event is what José Martí had lived and died for.

During his short life, Martí was an editor, teacher, lawyer, philosopher and political activist; however, to Cubans, his eloquent poems, speeches and writings rallying for Cuban independence made him a national hero.

George Sims Monument

Address: Sims Park, 6341 Bank Street, New Port Richey. Phone: (800) 842–1873. Pasco County.

New Port Richey resident George Sims was a land developer in the early 1920s, a time when real estate was booming in the Sunshine State.

While vacationing in Great Neck, New York, Sims and his wife Marjorie befriended several celebrities, one of whom was silent-screen actor Thomas Meighan, notes the West Pasco Historical Society Museum.

Sims apparently captivated these celebrities with his description of New Port Richey's year-round warm climate, semi-tropical landscape and scenic Cotee River, because Meighan accepted Sims' invitation to visit the city. The American actor built a house overlooking the Cotee River.

Soon, other celebrities built neighboring homes along the Cotee or frequently visited the town. Notables who flocked

George Sims Monument, Sims Park. Photo provided by Pasco County Office of Tourism.

to New Port Richey included actor-vaudevillian Ed Wynn, bandleader Paul Whiteman, ballplayer Babe Ruth and golfer Gene Sarazen.

As a real-estate developer, Sims probably realized that if famous stars built homes in New Port Richey, the city would potentially earn a reputation as a movie colony. He was right—for a while.

Sims donated land to New Port Richey with a proviso that it be used as parkland for the enjoyment of the residents. That parcel of land was originally called Enchantment Park. It is now known as Sims Park.

Sims Park hosts the Chasco Fiesta, an annual eleven-day springtime event that began in 1922. Centering on Native American history and legend, the fiesta features the crowning of a Queen Chasco. In 1922, that title was bestowed on Sims' wife, Marjorie.

The eight-acre park presents concerts at its amphitheater, and the Cotee River Seafood Fest and Boat Show takes place every Mother's Day weekend at and near the Park.

George W. Bush gave a speech at Sims Park during his second presidential campaign. A plaque at the park commemorates Bush's visit.

The West Pasco Historical Society Museum is on the grounds of Sims Park. The museum is housed in the former Seven Springs schoolhouse, a two-room building that dates to the early 1900s.

George Sims died in 1954 at the age of seventy-eight. Initially, he was buried in his namesake park, but his remains were eventually removed to a cemetery.

There is a monument to George Sims in Sims Park at the spot where he was originally interred. The monument, overlooking Orange Lake, is about four feet high and is covered with small round stones and large pebbles that frame a plaque. The plaque is inscribed:

George Sims. Founder of New Port Richey. 1876–1954.

As the developer of New Port Richey, Sims brought civilization to a largely uninhabited area. He also is remembered as a man whose influence and persuasiveness made New Port Richey glitter with glamour.

Treasured Memories of New Port Richey Mural

Address: Carl Reef Building, 6307 Grand Boulevard, New Port Richey. (727) 847–8129. Pasco County.

In the early part of the twentieth century, New Port Richey had a connection to Hollywood and the movies.

That connection is memorialized in a downtown mural titled *Treasured Memories of New Port Richey*. It was painted by local artist Tamara Gerkin in 2005.

The mural captures famous residents and visitors at the Meighan Theatre, the Hacienda Hotel, and other local landmarks.

It pays tribute to the city's glamorous past, when stars of the silent-screen era lived in New Port Richey or visited there. These stars included Thomas Meighan, Gloria Swanson, Ed Wynn and Charlie Chaplin.

In 1925, actor Thomas Meighan built a home along the Pithlachascotee (Cotee) River, which runs through New Port Richey. Except for a gatehouse, his home no longer exists.

In 1925, a new five-hundred-seat movie theatre opened in New Port Richey. It was an elaborate brick building with

Treasured Memories of New Port Richey Mural.

Moorish design elements and columns imported from Italy. It was christened the Thomas Meighan Theatre. It operates today as the Richey Suncoast Theatre.

The locals must have swelled with pride to attend celebrity-studded screenings of Meighan's films, such as *The New Klondike* (1926), at the Thomas Meighan Theatre. He was, after all, a New Port Richey resident.

Tall, with wavy brown hair and matinee-idol good looks, Meighan was born in Pittsburgh in 1879. He began his acting career on the Broadway stage and eventually went to Hollywood to try his luck in the burgeoning film industry.

He attracted the attention and favor of famous producer-director Cecil B. DeMille, who cast him in successful silent movies including *The Trail of the Lonesome Pine* (1916) and *Male and Female* (1919).

One of Meighan's most critical successes was as a gangster in the 1919 silent film *The Miracle Man*, costarring Lon Chaney (Halliwell 1991). For more than a decade, Meighan reigned as one of Paramount Studios' biggest silent-screen actors.

He starred opposite popular actresses Gloria Swanson, Billie Burke (later the good witch Glinda in *The Wizard of Oz*), Blanche Sweet and Norma Talmadge.

With the rise of talkies, Meighan's popularity waned. His last role of note was in *Peck's Bad Boy* (1934), starring child actor Jackie Cooper.

In 1936, Thomas Meighan died from cancer at the age of fifty-seven. He and his wife, the former stage actress Frances Ring, had been married twenty-seven years. They had no children.

The mural in New Port Richey includes painted re-creations of the movie posters for *Male and Female*, in which Meighan co-starred with Gloria Swanson, and *Sunset Boulevard*, the critically acclaimed 1950 movie in which Swanson starred.

Swanson's connections to New Port Richey were her appearances in silent films with Thomas Meighan, her presence at movie premieres at the Meighan Theatre and, if you believe local lore, her rendezvous with Joseph P. Kennedy at the Hacienda Hotel when she was in town.

Books and movies have alluded to Swanson's affair with the father of John F. Kennedy, but at the time, her affair was hidden from the public.

Swanson was born in Chicago and began her career by playing one of Mack Sennett's bathing beauties. Her career spanned many decades and six husbands, the first of whom was Wallace Beery. Cecil B. DeMille directed her in six acclaimed films. She died in 1983 at the age of eighty-six.

Because New Port Richey was Florida's version of a movie colony, the 1927 Mediterranean Revival-style Hacienda Hotel, as depicted in the mural, hosted celebrity luminaries from Hollywood and New York.

Given the major films that premiered at the Meighan Theatre and the famous people who lived and visited there, New Port Richey could have become an enduring celebrity colony much like Malibu or the Hamptons, in New York. Three events thwarted that development.

The American stock market crashed in 1929. The Great Depression of the 1930s followed. Thomas Meighan died in 1936. For New Port Richey, it was the end of an era.

The *Treasured Memories of New Port Richey* mural is a reminder of the city's heyday, when glamour reigned.

Stewart "Stewy" Abramowicz Memorial

**Address: Pioneer Park, 6799 Pinehurst Drive, Spring Hill.
(1–800) 601–4580. Hernando County.**

Within Spring Hill's seven-acre Pioneer Park, there is a black granite monument that owes its existence to maternal love.

The six-foot-tall monument is dedicated to a boy named Stewy Abramowicz and it is the centerpiece of a 3½-acre section of Pioneer Park called Stewy's Skate Park.

The monument is inscribed:

> Stewy.
>
> Dedicated to the memory of Stewart 'Stewy' Abramow-icz, August 10, 1988–January 20, 2001, and to all the young people who worked beside him to make this dream a reality.
>
> Stewy, a skateboard enthusiast, dreamed of a skateboard park at Pioneer Park and began the wheels turning toward that end. His efforts were cut short by his tragic death, but his family, along with a group of his peers, picked up where Stewy left off.
>
> KIDS 4 Kids worked unselfishly for months, soliciting donations for the development of the skate park. They suc-ceeded. Stewy's dream is now a reality.

Inside the park, Amber Costa runs a food concession called Stewy's Snack Shack. Every day, she can watch kids skateboarding there. She can see the monument. That pleases her, because Amber Costa was Stewy's mother. This is Amber's story about herself, her son and a memorial to him.

On January 19, 2001, Costa's twelve-year-old twin sons, Stewart and Anthony, were riding together on a scooter past Pioneer Park. They were on their way to the grounds of an unoccupied neighborhood supermarket, where they could practice their skateboarding. Stewy was riding behind Anthony as Anthony pushed the scooter.

An eighty-year-old woman was driving down the street outside Pioneer Park. Costa says the woman's car plowed into the boys. Anthony suffered a blood clot to his brain.

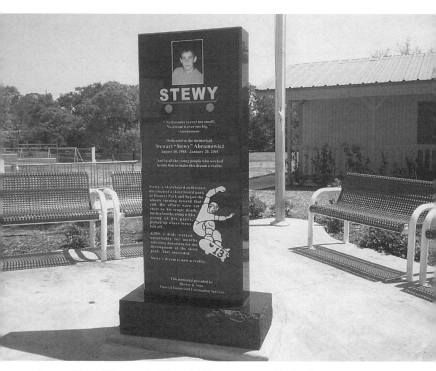

Stewart "Stewy" Abramowicz Memorial. Photo courtesy of Amber Costa.

Stewy was dragged 165 feet. Anthony eventually recovered. Stewy died.

"Stewy often said that he wanted a skate park to be built in Spring Hill, a place where he and his friends could skateboard," says Costa. Grief-stricken, she realized that for safety's sake, a skate park was a necessity. The children of Spring Hill realized it, too. But how could they make that happen?

One day, a ten-year-old girl rang Costa's doorbell. The girl held a bucket containing eight hundred dollars she had raised through donations. "Can we build a skate park?" the girl asked Costa.

Costa, several parents and dozens of skaters approached the Hernando County Commission to convince the members of the need for such a park. Stewart had already begun a petition for the park prior to his death. "Stewy had thought that if he collected enough signatures from local kids and parents, he'd be closer to his dream," Costa says. "Before his death, he had collected three hundred signatures."

Costa beseeched more people to sign the petition. Combined with Stewart's original three hundred, she ended up with more than three thousand signatures. Still, there seemed to be insufficient community support.

County Commissioner Diane Rowden's son had died in a swimming accident. She understood the importance to Costa of building a skate park and how it would keep Stewy's memory alive. She was on Costa's side.

Costa says that she and those who rallied behind her raised about $142,000 from fundraisers and donations, and the commission agreed to provide matching funds.

Rowden and Costa organized a group called KIDS 4 Kids. These youngsters not only raised money, they eventually pitched in to design the skate park's modular equipment. Companies donated building materials.

The monument's public unveiling in 2003 is an event Costa remembers vividly. On that day it was raining across the street, but the sun was shining down on the monument "like a circle around the park, like a miracle in that one spot," she says.

The likeness of Stewart Abramowicz that is etched into the granite monument resembles a color photograph.

A skateboarder is etched onto the front of the monument. A similar figure, with a number 13 on his helmet—Stewy's football jersey number was 13—is etched onto the back of the monument.

Costa says that before Stewy died, he and Anthony made a pact to go skydiving together someday. The twin brothers also planned to join the Air Force together. Those dreams have died, but not Stewy's dream of a skate park.

Today, between fifty and seventy-five skateboarding youths may show up at the skate park during the week. About 150 of them skate there on weekends. The park is safe. It is their place. Because of a mother's love, Stewy's dream came true.

Amber Costa is certain that Stewy is looking down from heaven and smiling. She glances toward the monument. "He hasn't gone anywhere," she says. "He's still here."

Central Florida

Memorial to Emil Billitz, Sr., and the CCC Workers

Address: **Highlands Hammock State Park, 5931 Hammock Road, Sebring. (863) 386–6094. Highlands County.**

In 1933, when the nation was in the throes of an economic depression, President Franklin D. Roosevelt initiated a government program, the Civilian Conservation Corps (CCC).

The CCC, which lasted until 1943, was created to provide employment for young men between the ages of eighteen and twenty so that they would not be forced to go on relief. They signed up for a minimum of six months' work.

The CCC workers were paid one dollar per day. At the end of each month, they were permitted to keep five dollars, but they had to send home the remaining twenty-five dollars to help support their families.

The CCC Museum at Highlands Hammock State Park in Sebring uses photographic murals, interpretive panels and artifacts to convey the story of the CCC.

According to Darrel Smith, a park ranger/historian at Highlands Hammock State Park, the CCC workers restored America's infrastructure with little more than a pick, a shovel and an axe.

They hauled materials in dump trucks, cleared pathways, built sewers and roads and planted thousands of plants in state parks around the country. Worker Emil Billitz was part of this story.

Outside the museum, a six-foot-tall, six-hundred-pound bronze statue representing a CCC volunteer stands atop a

Memorial to Emil Billitz, Sr., and the CCC Workers.

stone base with a plaque in it. The bare-chested figure holds
the handle of a shovel in his right hand.

The CCC statue at Highlands Hammock State Park was
installed by Henry Billitz, a former CCC worker, in memory
of his brother Emil, who joined the CCC in 1942.

The plaque beneath the statue reads:

Dedicated to the memory of Emil Billitz, Sr., and countless other CCC enrollees who were injured, disabled or lost their lives in performance of their duty. We especially remember the 228 CCC members who perished September 2, 1935, during a hurricane at three camps, Upper Keys, Florida.

Emil Billitz's granddaughter Kellie Blanco is a young schoolteacher in St. Augustine. She speaks endearingly about her grandfather's life.

Emil Billitz was born in Newark, New Jersey, in 1924. He was one of thirteen children born to German immigrants.

In 1942, at age eighteen, Billitz was working for the CCC when his truck went off the side of a mountain. His injuries made him a paraplegic.

Billitz spent a year in a hospital. He never regained use of his legs. With determination, he trained himself to walk on crutches rather than use a wheelchair. He didn't rely on a wheelchair until his later years.

When Billitz was twenty-five, his mother died. She had helped him care for his two young children. After her death he lost custody of his children.

"He was a devoted grandfather with a cheerful disposition," Blanco says. "I fondly remember him taking me on a road trip from Florida to Niagara Falls. We went to the World Trade Center, the Statue of Liberty and Washington, D.C.

"He loaded me and ten of my friends in his van to take us roller skating for my birthday. He was at every dance recital, school program or church play I was in. He was a remarkable man. I was honored to have him in my life."

When Blanco entered college in 1995, Billitz drove from St. Augustine to Gainesville once a week to see her. He was self-educated and believed very strongly in education, and under his influence she became a teacher.

Billitz worked at odd jobs—factory work, a paper route— but many places wouldn't hire him because of his disability.

In 1996, at age seventy-two, Emil Billitz died from a heart attack. He is buried in St. Augustine.

Chief Chipco Monument

Address: Sample Park, U.S. 27, north of S.R. 542, Lake Hamilton. Polk County.

In reminiscing about his part in the Seminole Indian Wars, the Tallahassee chief named Chipco reportedly stated that his only regret was that he tossed a white infant in the air, then caught it with the tip of his hunting knife.

This startling statement appeared in an article by writer Spessard Stone (*Herald Advocate*, January 1, 2004).

Given that Chief Chipco admitted to having committed at least one atrocity, why, then, should there be a monument dedicated to him in a park in Lake Hamilton?

The answer can be found in the monument's inscription:

> In memory of Chief Chipco. Lover of Peace. Friend of the White Man. His Seminole Indian village was located on Boner's Island in Lake Hamilton 1855. Dedicated by Ponce de Leon Chapter, Daughters of the American Revolution, Winter Haven, Florida 1957.

The Seminole Wars killed innocent people on both sides of the conflict as the white man sought to remove the Native Americans to reservations west of the Mississippi River and as the tribes defended their freedom and their land.

Chipco claimed to have been among the attacking warriors in the Dade Massacre of 1835, which killed Major Francis Dade and nearly all of Dade's men. The chief was involved in other attacks, as well.

According to "Chipco and Tallahassee led Seminole Remnant in Florida," an article by Albert DeVane that appeared in the *Tampa Tribune* on July 15, 1956, General Andrew Jackson's troops galloped into a Seminole camp at Suwannee during the First Seminole War (around 1818) and killed Chipco's father.

By later attacking the white man, perhaps Chipco was avenging his own loss and the cruelties he had seen the white man perpetrate on Native Americans.

After Jackson defeated the Creeks in the Battle of Horseshoe Bend (1814), some of the tribe members, including

Chief Chipco Monument.

Chief Osceola, Francis the Prophet and Chief Chipco, sought refuge in Florida.

Chipco and his band lived around the Aucilla River in northwest Florida, in the vicinity of Tallahassee. They then moved south to areas around Tampa and Ocala. Chipco was from the Tallahassee tribe of the Red Stick Upper Creeks. He was born in Alabama around 1801 and died in 1881.

The *Tampa Tribune* article describes Chipco as being broad-shouldered and nearly six feet tall. In his later life, he greeted his white friends with the words, "my friend, my friend," and he punctuated his words with a smile. He had a robust laugh and enjoyed telling tales about his many hunting experiences.

Chipco was married twice. He had no children to carry his name, but his nephew, Tallahassee, had nine children, one of whom he named Chipco II. Chipco's second wife was Tallahassee's sister.

In the 1850s, Plant City was a Native American town called Echebucsassa or Ichepuckesassa. Chipco and his band were then living in Central Florida, and the chief often camped in Echebucsassa and visited white friends before continuing on to Fort Brooke (Tampa) to trade hides and beads, notes the Florida chapter of the Daughters of the American Revolution (DAR).

In the mid-1850s, a white friend warned Chipco that a company of the Florida Militia planned to capture the chief and his band and remove them from Florida. The militiamen found only an abandoned camp. Chipco was gone.

Near the end of Chipco's life, he passed his title, chief of the Cow Creek Seminoles, to his nephew Tallahassee.

On November 12, 1881, the *Bartow Courier-Informant* reported that Chipco had died the previous month and that he had been buried with his rifle and hunting equipment.

According to Willard S. Steele, tribal historic preservation officer, Seminole Tribe of Florida, Tallahassee moved Chipco's band south, where they settled around Palm Beach and up through Martin County until the Brighton Reservation was created.

The Cow Creek Seminoles who now live on the Brighton Reservation in Florida are descendants of the Creek Indians who lived in Georgia and Alabama.

August Heckscher Monument

Address: Crystal Lake Park, N. Lake Shore Boulevard and Orange Avenue, Lake Wales. Polk County.

August Heckscher lived the American dream. His life was a rags-to-riches story that probably evolved through a combination of good luck and great business acumen. He embodied the spirit of capitalism and philanthropy.

Many New Yorkers will immediately recognize the name August Heckscher.

Long Island's August Heckscher Museum of Art, in Huntington, and Heckscher State Park, near East Islip, are named for him. So is the Heckscher Foundation, in Manhattan. Why, then, is there a monument in Crystal Lake Park that bears this New York philanthropist's name?

The answer is, he loved children. In 1921, he created Heckscher Foundation for Children, which promotes the welfare of underprivileged youth.

Heckscher donated playground equipment to parks and, although he lived in New York, he owned a winter home

August Heckscher Monument.

and orange groves near Lake Wales, so Crystal Lake Park became one of the beneficiaries of his generosity.

Inside the park, adjacent to the playground, there is a stone monument bearing these words:

> August Heckscher. Donated the original playground equipment in the 1930s, then rebuilt the park in the 1950s. This marker stands as a memorial to his gift. Lake Wales Parks Department.

The Heckscher Museum of Art provides the following information about August Heckscher.

He was born in Hamburg, Germany, in 1848. When he was nineteen, he took his savings of five hundred dollars and sailed to New York.

Heckscher worked during the day and studied English at night. He and his cousin Richard formed a coal-mining company, Richard Heckscher & Company, which they later sold to the Philadelphia-Reading Railroad.

Heckscher then established the Zinc and Iron Company, which later became New Jersey Zinc Company. He went on to form the Vermont Copper Company.

By the early 1900s, Heckscher had turned his sights to real estate. He formed a realty corporation through which he bought property around New York. He owned more than eighty acres in Huntington Harbor and lived there for many years.

In 1917, Heckscher purchased 18.5 acres of land in Huntington that had been the site of a thimble factory. He hired a landscape architect to design a park for children. Then, he hired an architectural firm to design the fine arts building, today known as Heckscher Museum of Art.

At a ceremony on July 10, 1920, Heckscher dedicated the park and the museum to the people of Huntington. He liked artists of the Hudson River School, and the museum still houses many works by artists representing that American art movement.

In addition to creating parks and playgrounds for underprivileged children in New York, Heckscher sponsored summer camps for poor youths and shipped citrus to them from his groves in Polk County.

The May 1, 1941, edition of the *Lake Wales News* featured a front-page article about the life and death of August Heckscher.

He married his first wife, Anna Atkins, of Pottsville, Pennsylvania, in 1881. She died in 1924. Their daughter Antoinette became Lady Ester, of London, England. His grandson, also named August, became New York City parks commissioner in the 1960s.

Heckscher died at his home in Polk County in 1941 at the age of ninety-two. He was survived by his children and his second wife. He was buried at Woodlawn Cemetery, in the Bronx. He made life a playground for thousands of children.

Major General E. M. Law Monument

Address: Corner of Summerlin Street and Broadway, Bartow. Polk County.

Were it not for an ex-Confederate general named E. M. Law, would there be a University of Florida as we know it?

According to Downtown Bartow, Inc.'s brochure, "Historic Bartow: A Self-Guided Tour to the Grandeur of Yesteryear," General Law established the South Florida Military Institute in Bartow in 1894. It later became part of University of Florida.

"Gen. E. M. Law, Ranking Confederate Officer, Is Dead," ran the headline of an article published in the November 2, 1920, edition of the *Polk County Record*. The article reported that when Evander McIvor Law died in Bartow on Sunday, October 31, 1920, he was the last surviving major general of the Southern armies.

According to the article, Law was so revered that George W. Oliver, mayor of Bartow, issued the following proclamation, calling for the community to show its love and esteem for General Law:

> I . . . request that all business . . . be suspended and business houses closed during the hour from three o'clock to four o'clock on the Second Day of November, A.D. 1920, as a token of our respect, love and esteem of General Law.

That day in Polk County, students filed into their school auditoriums to hear memorials to Law before being dismissed for the afternoon. Many went to the cemetery to attend Law's burial.

On November 2, the Polk County Record published a photo of Law, showing him with a mustache and a full beard. Next to his photo, the newspaper declared: "The South suffers a loss . . . military funeral is being largely attended this afternoon . . . tribute in floral offerings magnificent."

Today, a stone monument stands on the corner of Summerlin Street and Broadway in front of a Wachovia Bank. The monument is inscribed with these words:

This memorial marks the home, from 1904 until his death in 1920, of Maj. Gen. E. M. Law, CSA.

In addition to Law's former home, two local buildings connected to him still exist. The brick E. A. Law Building at 310–318 Main Street was built in 1907. The wood frame building at 1140 S. Broadway that housed the South Florida Military Institute is now a private residence.

The Polk County Historical and Genealogical Library is located in the elegant old courthouse in Bartow. Here, among the files, a newspaper obituary chronicles Law's life.

The name of the newspaper and the date of the obituary are not identified, but beneath the title, "Maj. Gen. E. M. Law Dead; Polk County Loses Distinguished Citizen," the clipping provides this information:

Evander McIvor Law was born in Darlington, South Carolina, in 1836. After graduating from South Carolina Military Academy, he became a teacher. He then moved to Tuskegee, Alabama, to open a military school.

Major General E. M. Law Monument.

As a Confederate officer during the Civil War, Law fought with the Fourth Alabama regiment, was wounded at Manassas and rose through the ranks, commanding a brigade as he fought again at Manassas and then Antietam and Fredericksburg. He also led a division at Gettysburg.

General James Longstreet commended Law for his command at Chicamauga. Law was wounded at Cold Harbor. After his recovery, he served for a time as General Joseph E. Johnston's chief of staff.

After the war, in addition to founding the South Florida Military Institute, Law became editor of the Bartow *Courier-Informant*, a position he held until his retirement in 1915. Law is buried at Oak Hill Cemetery in Bartow.

Billy Makinson and Nathaniel Carson Memorial

Address: 200 Lakeshore Boulevard, Kissimmee. Osceola County.

In the walkway toward the Makinson-Carson post of the American Legion, Post 10, there is a royal blue post that resembles a lamppost.

Perched on top is a globe bearing the logo of the American Legion; words underneath reveal that the post is a memorial to two young soldiers from Kissimmee:

> In memory.
> Billie Makinson.
> St. Mihiel.
> 1918.
> Nat Carson.
> The Argonne.
> November 1918.

The name "Billie" is spelled incorrectly. According to Dave Fopiano, past commander of Makinson-Carson Post 10, Billy Makinson was the first soldier from Kissimmee to die in World War I. He was promoted to the rank of second lieutenant shortly before his death.

Billy Makinson and Nathaniel Carson Memorial.

Makinson was killed at St. Mihiel, a town in northeast France, along the Meuse River, which had been captured by the Germans. In September 1918, it was recaptured by American troops.

It seems tragic, if not ironic, that Makinson died less than two months before the armistice was declared that ended World War I. In the United States, thereafter, Armistice Day became an annual holiday of remembrance and was eventually renamed Veterans Day.

Makinson died on unfamiliar soil in one of the most brutal battles of the First World War. He perished a continent away from his lifelong home in the cattle-ranching, boat-building community of Kissimmee, along the shores of Lake Tohopekaliga.

According to Billy's relatives, Buster and Bill Makinson, Billy was the eldest of fourteen children. He had two brothers and eleven sisters. Billy was tall and slender, serious-minded and patriotic, and it was probably soon after his graduation from high school that he joined the Fifth Infantry.

The Makinson name is firmly entrenched in Kissimmee history. Billy's father was William B. Makinson, Sr., who moved from Maryland to Kissimmee in 1882 to help his brother Carroll run the local hardware store on E. Broadway Avenue.

In 1884, William B. Makinson, Sr., took over Makinson's Hardware Store. Succeeding generations of Makinsons continue to operate the store, which they believe is the oldest extant hardware store in Florida.

The American Legion's Makinson-Carson Post 10 was established in 1923 and is named in honor of Billy Makinson and Nathaniel Carson, both of whom died while fighting on the Western Front.

Fopiano says that Nathaniel Carson, Company L, Fifth Marines, was the second soldier from Kissimmee to die in World War I. He died in a district of northeast France called the Argonne, the scene of the largest U.S. engagement in the war. He was killed eighteen days after Billy Makinson died at St. Mihiel.

Monument of States

Address: Corner of Monument Avenue and Johnston Street, Kissimmee. Osceola County.

The Monument of States was built as a tourism gimmick and it surely must be one of Florida's strangest attractions.

The forty-foot-high pyramid-shaped monument is built of stones affixed to blocks of cement. The stones come from the forty-eight continental states, plus twenty foreign countries, notes the Kissimmee Convention and Visitors Bureau. (Alaska and Hawaii were not states when the monument was built.)

Monument of States.

The genesis of the monument can be traced to a Kissimmee physician named Charles Bressler-Pettis, who had collected many of these stones during his travels. As president of the Kissimmee All-States Tourist (KAST) club, Bressler-Pettis collaborated with his fellow KAST members on the idea creating a unique monument to attract tourists to Kissimmee.

In addition to designing the monument, Bressler-Pettis sculpted the striking work of art that crowns it: an eagle with a six-foot wingspan sitting on a blue concrete ball. Bressler-Pettis' ashes are buried at the front of the monument.

The eclectic monument was dedicated in 1943 by U.S. Senator Claude Pepper. The 1,500 natural and manmade objects that form the pyramid include bricks, petrified wood, meteors and stalagmites. The stones were donated by tourists, governors, a prime minister, and a president of the United States.

Each state's stone is inscribed with the name of whomever was governor at the time the stone was donated, including Ohio governor John Bricker (1941) and Florida governor Spessard L. Holland (1941).

About twenty-two narrow rows of stones wrap around the monument. They are reinforced with steel rails. The monument weighs about sixty thousand pounds, notes the Kissimmee Convention and Visitors Bureau.

The monument includes fragments of stone from the Washington Monument, in Washington, D.C., plus one stone that from a distance appears to say "KISS MEE." Come closer and you'll see that it says "KISSimMEE."

You will need a zoom lens or binoculars to read the stones at the highest rows.

In addition to the state stones, the monument features stones etched with outlines of a map of the United States, a buffalo, a star (representing Texas) and a palm tree, among others. The highest stone is inscribed "unique."

That's certainly an apt description of the Monument of States.

Knowles Memorial Chapel

Address: Rollins College, 1000 Holt Avenue, Winter Park. (407) 646–2115. Orange County.

With its stunning Spanish classical-style architecture and its religious tapestries and paintings, Knowles Memorial Chapel may be the most beautiful building on the campus of Rollins College, in Winter Park.

The chapel was designed by Boston architect Ralph Adams Cram, who also designed the Cathedral of St. John the Divine in New York City and the chapel at West Point.

Frances Knowles Warren funded the building of the chapel as a memorial to her father, Francis Bangs Knowles. The chapel was dedicated on March 29, 1932.

One week later, also in memory of their father, Frances' sister Mabel gifted the chapel with a Skinner pipe organ, made by the Skinner Organ Company of Boston, noted the June 1921 *Rollins Alumni Record*.

Knowles Memorial Chapel.

In February 1935, Rollins College issued the booklet "Francis Bangs Knowles, Philanthropist and Lover of Youth" to coincide with the school's semi-centennial.

The booklet was supervised by Frances Knowles Warren "in loving memory of her Father, and to Commemorate his Generous Contribution . . . to the . . . College."

Francis Bangs Knowles was born on November 29, 1823, in Harwick, Massachusetts. He could trace his ancestry to a Revolutionary War soldier and to a signer of the Declaration of Independence.

In 1845, he became a manufacturer of men's clothing and gloves. Little more than fifteen years later, the Union Army would be wearing his company's buckskin gloves.

Also in 1845, two days before Christmas, he married Ann Eliza Poole of Gloversville, New York. Ann Eliza died in 1865.

In the spring of 1867, Knowles married Hester Greene of Worcester, who bore him two daughters, Mabel and Frances, and two sons. Knowles also had a son and daughter from his marriage to Ann Eliza.

By 1862, Knowles and his brother Lucius were entrenched in a business that built steam pumps and looms. It grew into Knowles Looms Works, headquartered in Worcester.

Knowles was a philanthropist, making generous donations in support of local charities and organizations. He spread his generosity not only in Massachusetts, but also in Winter Park, Florida, his winter home.

In 1883, Knowles visited Winter Park for the first time and invested in the building of the Seminole Hotel there. It opened one year later.

Knowles became president of the Winter Park Company, which developed the town as a winter resort. From the construction of churches and schools to the planting of oak trees to line the streets, Knowles put his philanthropic stamp on Winter Park and on Rollins College.

According to the semi-centennial booklet, the directors of the Orlando and Winter Park Railway, of which Knowles was president, resolved that they would "ever hold in highest appreciation his kindness and generosity, his pure and spotless character, his noble traits and sagacious advice."

Knowles became a major benefactor of Rollins College, serving on the first board of trustees and financing the construction of several buildings on campus.

Knowles died in Washington, D.C., on May 15, 1890. His motto had been, "The world shall be better for my having passed through it."

Linton E. Allen Memorial Fountain

Address: Lake Eola Park, 195 N. Rosalind Avenue, Orlando. Orange County.

What is that huge water-spouting object in the middle of Lake Eola, visitors often wonder? A flying saucer? An alien spaceship? A giant Jell-O mold?

None of the above. The mystery object is, in fact, the Linton E. Allen Memorial Fountain.

In May 1965, Linton Allen, president of the First National Bank in Orlando, was attending Sunday church services when he suddenly died. He was seventy-six years old.

Soon after Allen's death, local officials voted to re-name a local landmark in his honor. The Orlando Centennial Fountain, completed in 1957 for $162,000, was christened Linton E. Allen Memorial Fountain (*Orlando Sentinel,* October 27, 1983, 1F).

The fountain began as an idea in Allen's head. He was traveling in Europe in 1955 and admiring the beautiful foun-

Linton E. Allen Memorial Fountain.

tains he saw in England, Spain and Italy, when a thought struck him. Why shouldn't Orlando have a similar fountain?

Back home he dashed off a letter to the editor (*The Star*, June 18, 1955) and met with civic leaders. Together with the Orlando Utility Commission and the mayor, they set in motion a plan to construct a fountain in the middle of Lake Eola.

According to an article written by Jeff Kunerth, Atlanta landscape architect W. C. Pauley was paid $1,200 to design Centennial Fountain (*Orlando Sentinel*, October 27, 1983).

Furthermore, at the dedication ceremony, the fountain was filled with a mix of various waters from Lake Eola and fountains in Spain, England, France, Alabama and Washington, D.C.

This blend of waters symbolized the five flags that had flown over Florida: Spanish, British, French, Confederate and the United States.

An article published in the *Orlando Sentinel* on January 4, 2004, describes the fountain's vital statistics:

The dome is made of green Plexiglas panels. The fountain works via a system of pumps, fifty-one water jets, one of which can spout seventy-five feet high, an 87,000-volt lighting system, a computer that regulates the fountain's jet sequences and color changes and assorted electrical equipment.

It took about three hundred tons of concrete to build the fountain, which sits on twenty-six pylons, each sixty feet tall. More than five million gallons of water swirl through the fountain each day.

Nobody is certain how Lake Eola got its name. One legend claims that in the 1870s, the son of pioneer cattleman Jacob Summerlin named the lake for his fiancée, who died of typhoid fever.

What is certain is that the fountain fulfills Linton Allen's dream for Orlando.

Orlando Reeves Monument

Address: Southeast corner of Lake Eola Park, 195 N. Rosalind Avenue, Orlando. Orange County.

Beneath an oak tree in Lake Eola Park, Orlando, rests a weathered stone with a plaque. The words on the monument read:

> Orlando Reeves. In whose honor our city Orlando was named. Killed in this vicinity by Indians September 1835.
> Erected by the students of Cherokee Junior High School 1939.

Was the city of Orlando really named for Orlando Reeves, some visitors might wonder? Did Orlando Reeves ever exist? These questions have never been answered.

In 1854, Judge James G. Speer migrated to central Florida from South Carolina. He was instrumental in the selection of Orlando as the seat of Orange County.

Speer also had a hand in naming the city, as described by author Eve Bacon in her book *Orlando: A Centennial His-*

Orlando Reeves Monument.

tory. Legend has it Speer was a fan of Shakespeare's works and wanted the city to be named for the character Orlando in *As You Like It*.

Alternate versions of the story, according to Bacon, claim that Judge Speer named the city after one of his employees, or that Orlando was named for Orlando Rees, a landowner in Volusia County, which was formed from Orange County.

However, the most persistent and widely accepted story is that Orlando was named in memory of a soldier who was killed by Seminoles during the Second Seminole War.

Bacon presents us with a question mark. If federal government archives list not one army soldier named Orlando Reeves among the officers and soldiers who died in the Seminole Wars, how did the following story originate?

One night in September 1835, Reeves, along with other federal soldiers and volunteers, made camp along what is now Lake Eola.

While on sentinel duty, Reeves spotted what looked like a log in the lake. The log seemed to be rolling slowly toward shore. Reeves suddenly realized that this was no log. This was a Seminole warrior stealthily approaching the camp.

Reeves fired his gun, alerting the soldiers. Then he fell, mortally wounded by an arrow shot by the Seminole. Reeves' fellow soldiers buried him nearby at a spot subsequently called Orlando's Grave.

According to Orlando historian Kena Fries, one account of Reeves describes him as having been "tall, lanky, wiry and dark-complected . . . quick on the trigger" (1938). If Reeves didn't exist, how could such a detailed description have been possible?

To add to the puzzle, there is another lingering story about the origins of the city's name, notes an online fact book about Orlando. Supposedly, a man named Mr. Orlando was on his way to Tampa when he took sick and died. Some locals buried him near where he took his last breath. Thereafter, people would point to the grave and say, "There lies Orlando" (ColombiaLink.com).

In an article for *Metro* magazine, writer Pepper Mueller describes the city of Orlando's beginnings as a small settlement called Jernigan.

It was named for Captain Aaron Jernigan, who owned a cattle ranch in Sanford, then part of the sprawling Mosquito County (Orange County's original name).

So, we come back to the puzzling questions: How did Orlando get its name? Was it named for Orlando Reeves? *Was* there an Orlando Reeves?

The students of Cherokee Junior High School who erected the monument in Lake Eola Park obviously were partial to the bravest of the legends.

Dade Battlefield Historic State Park

Address: 7200 C.R. 603, S. Battlefield Drive, Bushnell. (352) 793–4781. Sumter County.

It was three days after Christmas in 1835. In a forest of pine flat woods, Major Francis Langhorne Dade tried to cheer up the 107 weary, cold soldiers in his command. They consisted of detachments of the Fourth Infantry, Second and Third Artillery.

"Have a good heart; our difficulties and dangers are over now, and as soon as we arrive at Fort King you'll have three days to rest and keep Christmas gaily," he told them.

Before the day was over, forty-three-year-old Major Dade would be dead, leaving a grieving widow and child in Pensacola.

The complete story of what happened on that day nearly 175 years ago can be found at the Dade Battlefield Historic State Park. A park ranger and a roomful of interpretive panels at the visitor center bring the tale to life.

Dade and his soldiers were traveling from Fort Brooke (Tampa) to Fort King, near Ocala, to strengthen the troops there, in anticipation of retaliation from the Seminoles. The Seminoles were angered by the federal government's order that they leave Florida.

Led by Micanopy, about 180 Seminoles converged on the Dade party, killing Dade and all but three of his men. The Seminoles lost only three warriors. The event came to be known as "Dade's Massacre" or the Dade Massacre.

The first white soldiers killed were Major Dade, a native of King George County, Virginia, and Captain Upton S. Fraser. Among the other fallen soldiers was twenty-nine-year-old Lieutenant William E. Basinger, of Savannah, Georgia, in whose name General Zachary Taylor established Fort Basinger along the Kissimmee River in 1837, almost two years to the day Basinger died.

Of the few survivors of the Dade Massacre, Private Edwin DeCourcy, a twenty-seven-year-old native of Maidstone, England, lay unconscious from his wounds.

Twenty-three-year-old Private Ransom Clarke, from Livingston, New York, also was injured. He revived DeCourcy,

Major Francis Dade
Monument, Dade
Battlefield Historic
State Park.

and together they slowly headed to Fort Brooke; however,
en route, DeCourcy was killed by a Seminole.

Clarke escaped and crawled his way to Fort Brooke.
Because of his injuries, he was discharged from further military duty. He supplemented his invalid's pension by booking
speaking engagements about the battle. He died five years
after the Dade Massacre. He was only twenty-eight.

The third survivor, thirty-two-year-old private Joseph
Sprague, a native of Washington, Vermont, hid in a pond
by the battle site. When the Seminole warriors had gone,
he made his way to Fort Brooke in spite of a broken arm.
Private Clarke had arrived at the fort one day earlier.

Among those taken captive by the Seminoles was Louis
Pacheco, Major Dade's African American interpreter. Two
years later, Pacheco surfaced among a group of Indians
whom the government had ordered to go west.

When former Seminole fighter General Edmund Gaines
(for whom the town of Gainesville was named) heard about
the Dade massacre, he put on his uniform again and set out
to reinforce Fort King.

En route with 1,100 men, he stopped at the Dade Massacre site and held a burial service. For seven weeks, the ambushed soldiers in Dade's command had lain where they died.

"Gracious God, what a sight!" Lieutenant James Duncan was quoted as exclaiming when he saw all the decaying bodies being preyed upon by hovering vultures.

The officers killed in the Dade Massacre were buried in individual graves on the east side of the battleground. The ninety-eight enlisted men were buried in two mass graves within the breastworks.

The Seminoles had thrown the command's cannon into a pond. Gaines' men pulled it out of the water and mounted it, muzzle down, in front of the officers' graves as a monument to them.

The ambush of Major Dade and his men segued into the Second Seminole War (1835–42), also known as the Seven Years War. It is considered the longest and costliest of our country's Indian wars.

Dade City, Florida, and Dade County, Florida, were named in the major's honor, as were Dade County, Missouri; Dade County, Georgia; and Major Francis Langhorne Dade County Courthouse, in Miami-Dade County.

On August 14, 1842, the remains of Major Dade and the other soldiers were re-interred in St. Augustine National Cemetery.

In 1972, Dade Battlefield Historic State Park was added to the National Register of Historic Places under the listing of "Dade Battlefield Historic Memorial." The park is also a National Historic Landmark.

The monument to Major Francis Dade is a tapered white column about ten feet tall that stands on a rugged stone base. The plaque is inscribed, "Here Major Dade Fell." Two similar monuments have plaques inscribed, "Here Capt. Fraser Fell," and "Here Lieut. Mudge Fell."

A commemorative bronze plaque in front of the visitor center announces:

> This ground dedicated by the State of Florida as a memorial to those who died here as American soldiers.

Bibliography

Adams, Chuck, Steve Jacob, and Suzanna Smith. "What Happened after the Net Ban?" Document FE 123, Food and Resource Economics Department, Florida Cooperative Extension Service, Institute of Food and Agricultural Sciences, University of Florida. Published February 2000. Reviewed June 2003. http://edis.ifas.ufl.edu/FE123.

Air Art Northwest. Bibliographic information on Colin Kelly and other World War II fighter pilots accompanying online image of "The Legend of John Kelly," a lithograph by Robert Taylor. Air Art Northwest. http://www.airartnw.com/colinkellylegend.htm.

Akin, Edward N. *Flagler, Rockefeller Partner and Florida Baron.* Gainesville: University Press of Florida, 1991.

Allen, Maury. "Jackie Robinson: An American Hero." *Eve's Magazine,* 1999. http://www.evesmag.com/robinson.htm.

American Civil War.com. "Natural Bridge: Civil War Florida." American Civil War.com. http://americancivilwar.com/statepic/fl/fl006.html.

Appleton's Encyclopedia. "David Rice Atchison." 1887. Copyright 2002 Virtualology. http://www.george-washington.org/davidatchison.com.

Astronauts Memorial Foundation. "Space Mirror Memorial." Astronauts Memorial Foundation. http://www.amfcse.org/space_mirror_memorial.htm.

Bacon, Eve. *Orlando: A Centennial History.* Chuluota, Fla.: Mickler House, 1975.

Battle of Olustee.org. "Fifty-fourth Massachusetts Infantry." Battle of Olustee.org. http://battleofolustee.org/54th_mass_inf.html.

Beaches of Fort Myers/Sanibel. "Arts, Culture and History in Pictures: Sgt. Clayton." Beaches of Fort Myers/Sanibel.com. http://www.fortmyerssanibel.com/cms/d/arts_culture_history_in_pictures.php.

Bridgwater, William, and Seymour Kurtz, eds. *Columbia Encyclopedia.* 3rd ed. New York: Columbia University Press, 1968.

Burnett, Gene M. *Florida's Past: People and Events That Shaped the State.* 3 vols. Sarasota: Pineapple Press, 1986.

———. "La Guantanamera." CasaCuba.org. http://www.casacuba.org.

Chapel, George L. "Dr. John Gorrie: Refrigeration Pioneer." Gorrie's Fridge. http://www.phys.ufl.edu/~ihas/gorrie/fridge.htm.

City of Lynn Haven, Florida. "The History of Lynn Haven, Florida." The City of Lynn Haven. http://www.cityoflynnhaven.com/history/history.htm.

———. "The Lynn Haven Monument." The City of Lynn Haven. http://www.cityoflynnhaven.com/history/memorial.htm.

ColombiaLink.com. "Orlando, Florida: Photos and Factbook." Colombia Link, USA City Factbooks. 2006. http://www.colombialink.com/usa/usa_cities/orlando.html.

Comer, Jane. "A Hero Remembered." *Madison Magazine,* Summer 1992, 15–17.

Covington, James W. *The Seminoles of Florida*. Gainesville: University Press of Florida, 1993.

Derr, Mark. *Some Kind of Paradise: A Chronicle of Man and the Land in Florida*. New York: William Morrow, 1989.

Downtown Fort Myers.com. "History." Downtown Fort Myers.com. 2007. http://www.downtownfortmyers.com/history.

Evans, Eli N. "The Confederacy." In *The Confederacy: MacMillan Information Now Encyclopedia*, edited by Richard N. Current. New York: MacMillan, 1998. Excerpted on Home of the American Civil War Web site. http://www.civilwarhome.com/benjaminbio.htm

———. *Judah P. Benjamin: The Jewish Confederate*. New York: Free Press, 1988.

Eversole, Chris. "UF Study: Net Ban Took a Bite, but Fishermen Recasting Themselves." *University of Florida News*, March 8, 1999. http://news.ufl. edu/1999/03/08/net-ban.

Finegan, Brig. General Joseph. "Reply of Brig. General Joseph Finegan, commanding Confederate Forces, to a letter from Brig. Gen. Seymour, commanding Federal Forces." Feb. 24, 1864. Official Records of the War of the Rebellion. Online at Battle of Olustee.org. http://battleofolustee. org/reports/finegan4.htm.

Florida Department of Military Affairs, Florida National Guard. "Camp Blanding Museum and Memorial Park: Installation and History." Camp Blanding Museum and Memorial Park official Web site. http://www. campblanding-museum.org/History.html.

Florida Society of American Foresters. "Austin Cary." Florida Society of American Foresters Hall of Fame. http://www.flsaf.org/hof.htm#hof-inductees.

Florida Supreme Court Historical Society. http://www.flcourthistory.com/ activitiesF.html.

Florida Supreme Court Library. http://library.flcourts.org.

Foster Hall Collection. "Stephen Collins Foster." Foster Hall Collection at the Center for American Music, University of Pittsburgh. http://www. pitt.edu/~amerimus/foster.htm.

Foundation for New Smyrna Museum of History. "Hidden Treasures, Historical Highlights of New Smyrna's Past." Edited by Dolores Maylone. Volusia Community History Site of Volusia County. http://volusia.com/ heritage/index.htm.

Fries, Kena. *Orlando in the Long, Long Ago . . . and Now*. Orlando: Ty Cobb's Florida Press, 1938.

Frisbee, John L. "Colin Kelly." *Air Force Magazine Online*. http://www.afa. org/magazine/valor/0694valor.asp.

Gaines, Kim. "Soldiers of Glory: U.S. Colored Troops in the Civil War. Black Collegian Online. http://www.black-collegian.com/african/sol-diers100.shtml.

Gannon, Michael. *Florida: A Short History*. Gainesville: University Press of Florida, 1993.

GlobalSecurity.org. "Camp Blanding/Fort Blanding: Starke, Florida." GlobalSecurity.org. http://www.globalsecurity.org/military/facility/camp-blanding.htm.

Green, Henry Alan, and Marcia Kerstein Zerivitz. *Mosaic: Jewish Life in*

Florida: A Documentary Exhibit from 1763 to the Present. Coral Gables: Mosaic, 1991.

Halliwell, Ruth, and John Walker. *Halliwell's Film Guide.* 8th ed. Edited by John Walker. London: HarperCollins, 1991.

Heller Bros. Packing Corp. "Hamlin Orange." Heller Bros. Packing Corp. 2003. http://www.hellerbros.com/hamlin_orange%20Description.htm.

J. N. "Ding" Darling Foundation. "Federal Duck Stamp Program." J. N. "Ding" Darling Foundation. 2000. http://www.ding-darling.org/stamp.html.

Kimball, Chris. "The Last Battle of the Third Seminole War." Originally published in *Florida Frontier Gazette*, Winter 2006. Online at Southern History: Tour of the Florida Territory during the Florida Seminole Wars, 1792–1859. http://www.southernhistory.us/palmhammock.htm.

Leonard, M. C. Bob. "Florida of the British." In *The Floridians: A Social History of Florida.* Florida History Internet Center. http://www.florida-history.org/floridians/british.htm.

———. "Florida of the Railroad Barons." In *The Floridians: A Social History of Florida.* Florida History Internet Center. http://www.floridahistory.org/floridians/railroad.htm.

———. "William D. Chipley." In *The Floridians: A Social History of Florida.* Florida History Internet Center. www.floridahistory.org/floridians/arch1/railroad/chipley2.htm.

McGoun, William. *Southeast Florida Pioneers: The Palm and Treasure Coasts.* Sarasota: Pineapple Press, 1998.

McIver, Stuart B. *Glimpses of South Florida History.* Miami: Florida Flair Books, 1988.

———. *Hemingway's Key West.* Sarasota: Pineapple Press, 1993.

Miller, Carlos. "A Young but Turbulent History." Magic City Media. http://www.magiccitymedia.com/HistoryofMiami.html.

Mueller, Pepper. "Orlando: the Legend Behind the Name." *Metro*, April 1993.

National Museum of the U.S. Air Force, Public Affairs. "Capt. Colin P. Kelly, Jr." National Museum of the U.S. Air Force. http://www.nationalmuseum.af.mil/factsheets/factsheet.asp?id=1598.

National Park Service. "Castillo de San Marco." www.nps.gov/casa.

———. "Fort Caroline National Memorial." www.nps.gov/foca.

Norwood's Restaurant and Wine Shop. "A Brief History of New Smyrna Beach." Norwood's Restaurant and Wine Shop. http://www.norwoods.com/welcome/NSB.html.

Okeeinfo. "Okeechobee Battlefield." Okeeinfo. 2002. Updated 2004. http://www.okeeinfo.com/okeeinfo_chapters/history/history_okee_okeechobee_battlefield.htm.

Parks, Arva Moore. *The Forgotten Frontier: Florida Through the Lens of Ralph Middleton Munroe.* Miami: Alfina Press, 1977.

Puma. "Brian's Life: A Song of Friendship, Courage." ESPN Online. http://espn.go.com/classic/biography/s/PiccoloBrian.html.

Reid, Thomas. *America's Fortress: A History of Fort Jefferson, Dry Tortugas, Florida.* Gainesville: University Press of Florida, 2006.

Rinhart, Floyd, and Marion Rinhart. *Victorian Florida: America's Last Frontier.* Atlanta: Peachtree, 1986.

Robert E. Lee Memorial Association. "Jessie Dew Ball du Pont." Robert E. Lee Memorial Association. http://www.stratfordhall.org/jbd.html ?RESEARCH.

Sandler, Roberta. *Guide to Florida Historical Walking Tours*. Sarasota: Pineapple Press, 1996.

Seymour, Truman. "Letter from Brig. Gen. Truman Seymour. Commanding Officer, U.S. Forces, District of Florida to Brig. Gen. Finegan, Commanding Officer, Confederate Forces, on the Engagement at Olustee, Florida, Concerning Union Wounded and Dead." Feb. 23, 1864. Official War Records of the Rebellion. Battle of Olustee.org. http://battleofolustee.org/reports/seymour2.htm.

Sixty-third Infantry Division Association. "Camp Blanding, Florida: Division Memorials, page 18." Sixty-third Infantry Division Association. http://www.63rdinfdiv.com/divisionmemorialspage18.html.

Southwest Florida Pioneers Historical Society. "Lee County Past to Present: History." Southwest Florida Pioneers Historical Society. 2002. http://www.rootsweb.com/~fllee/history/index.html.

State of Florida. "Constitution of 1838: Constitution or Form of Government for the People of Florida." Florida Constitution Revision Commission. http://www.law.fsu.edu/crc/conhist/1838con.html.

State of Florida, Department of Environmental Protection. "State to Acquire Historic Okeechobee Battlefield." Press release. April 4, 2006. Florida Department of Environmental Protection. http://www.dep.state.fl.us/secretary/news/2006/04/0404_01.htm.

State of Florida, Department of Environmental Protection, Division of Recreation and Parks. "Olustee Battlefield Historic State Park." Olustee Battlefield Historic State Park, Florida Online Park Guide. http://www.floridastateparks.org/olustee/default.cfm.

———. "Stephen Foster Folk Culture Center State Park History." Stephen Foster Folk Center State Park, Florida Online Park Guide. http://www.floridastateparks.org/stephenfoster/History.cfm.

State of Florida, Department of State. "The Battle of Natural Bridge." Florida in the Civil War: 1861–1865. http://www.flheritage.com/museum/mfh/exhibits/civilwar/18.cfm.

State of Florida, Florida Supreme Court. "Justice Richard W. Erwin." Supreme Court Portrait Gallery. http://www.floridasupremecourt.org/about/gallery/ervin.shtml.

St. Lucie Historical Society, Inc. Homepage. "Daniel T. McCarty." http://www.rootsweb.com/~flslchs/mccarty.htm.

Taylor, Roy. "Brian Piccolo Chicago Bears RB 1965–1969." Chicago Bears History site. 2002. http://www.bearshistory.com/lore/brianpiccolo.aspx.

Tebeau, Charlton W. *A History of Florida*. Coral Gables: University of Miami Press, 1971.

Time. "Silenced: A Calm Voice" (obituary of Dan McCarty). Time Magazine Online Archives. http://www.time.com/time/magazine/article/0,9171,860026,00.html.

University of Florida, Institute of Food and Agricultural Sciences. Document FE123, *UF Institute of Food and Agricultural Sciences*, February 2000.

University of Florida, School of Forest Resources and Conservation. "Pro-

256   Bibliography

file of Austin Cary." School of Forest Resources. http://www.sfrc.ufl.
edu/Facilities/acary.html.

U.S. Fish and Wildlife Service. "Jay Norwood "Ding" Darling." U.S. Fish
and Wildlife Service, J. N. 'Ding' Darling National Wildlife Refuge.
http://www.fws.gov/dingdarling/About/DingDarling.htm.

———. "Pelican Island National Wildlife Refuge." http://www.fws.gov/
pelicanisland/history.html.

U.S. Government. "The Indian Removal Act of 1830." Civics Online. http://
www.civics-online.org/library/formatted/texts/indian_act.html.

Wall of Americans. "CeeCee Lyles." http://www.wallofamericans.com/
php_files/wall.php?action=person_info&id=359.

Weeks, Dick (Shotgun). "The Price in Blood! Casualties in the Civil War."
Shotgun's Home of the American Civil War. http://www.civilwarhome.
com/casualties.htm.

Welch, Bob. "Unquestionably He Was a Hero." *Register Guard*, January 9,
2002.

West Florida Railroad Museum. "A Brief History: Pensacola and Atlantic Railroad." West Florida Railroad Museum. http://www.wfrm.org/
wfrmhistory.html.

Wiggins, Jim. *Glimpses of Florida's Past.* Kearns, Nebraska: Morris Publishing, 2002.

Woods, Chuck. "UF Extension Agent Says New Pickup Trucks in Cedar
Key Reflect Economic Impact of Clam Industry." *University of Florida
News,* April 10, 2006.

Index

Roberta Sandler is the author of *Guide to Florida Historical Walking Tours* (1996), which received the Florida Historical Society Golden Quill Award. She is a member of the Society of American Travel Writers and has written for publications such as the *New York Times*, *Chicago Tribune*, *Miami Herald*, *Baltimore Sun*, *Philadelphia Inquirer* and *San Diego Union-Tribune*.